INTEGRITY FIRST

America's Desperate Need for Leaders with Strong Moral Courage

J. Stark Davis

Dedication

This book is dedicated to the great Americans who fought and died for freedom in service to their country in Vietnam and Afghanistan. In honor, they gave their all for the cause of freedom from tyranny. In dishonor and disgrace, top U.S. government civilian and military leaders gave back to our nation's enemies all that so many Americans had paid for with their lives, blood, and sacrifice.

Table of Contents

Dedication 3

Introduction 6

Chapter 1: Lincoln's Strong Moral Leadership 13

Chapter 2: Integrity First 20

Chapter 3: The Border and Immigration 29

Chapter 4: The Federal (Non-)Budget 40

Chapter 5: The Right to Life 51

Chapter 6: The Afghanistan Withdrawal 68

Chapter 7: The Chinese Spy Balloon 78

Chapter 8: The HAMAS Terrorist Attack on Israel 81

Chapter 9: The United States Department of Justice 89

Chapter 10 United States Energy Policy 100

Chapter 11: Impeachment 105

Chapter 12: What is a Woman? 112

Chapter 13: Corporate America and International Trade 118

Chapter 14: Women in Combat 126

EPILOGUE 132

Acknowledgments 136

Exhibit A 137

About the Author 142

Notes.. **143**

Introduction

My motivation to write this book is driven by the dangerous failings of current leaders in America who are purposely and deceitfully leading our country away from our Christian foundation and into the very tyranny that our nation's original leaders fought to avoid. Our founders were escaping the heavy hand of monarchs who had taken away their freedoms in Europe and the American colonies. These early American leaders saw the dangers of men who ruled nations as tyrants. Our original leaders had the vision and the strength of character to stand against the king of England, and they designed a system of government with checks and balances to prevent power from getting into the hands of one, or a very few, men or women. Today we have a shortage of leaders with the courage to take a strong moral stand and defend our Constitution, which is designed to protect our fundamental freedoms. We are in a leadership crisis. Many people in leadership in big corporations, mass-media, education, and government think America's salvation is found in expansive government control over people's lives when the opposite is needed.

The leaders in our history who originally gave us this unique Republic back at the time of our revolution were leaders with strong moral courage. They were driven by a love for God and a love for freedom. They were strongly opposed to living under the rule of kings and queens who had the power to ruthlessly control people's lives and thoughts. This country was not formed by weak politicians seeking political power, it was formed by strong leaders willing to put their lives and prosperity on the line to take a stand for God-given rights. These rights began with the basic rights to life, liberty, and the pursuit of happiness. Our founding leaders knew the role of government must be purposely limited and checked with power balanced between the legislative, executive, and judicial branches. The limited government they left us was given the role of protecting fundamental freedoms through the rule of law, not through the rule of tyrants. The government was to be like a referee in an athletic contest to make sure the rules were followed, everyone was kept safe, and the game was played with fairness for all involved. The government was not to take the ball and play the game for people—it was up to each person to provide for themselves, to succeed or to fail.

I was raised in a small town in eastern Kentucky. Coming from a region known for its poverty, I am very aware of the continuum of cultural backgrounds found in this country. I am also aware that, no matter what the cultural heritage, people have become successful in America because they have chosen to enter the arena of competition, work hard, and honor God with the gifts they have been given. Over the years the U.S. government has created federal programs intended to help the poor and the elderly who may find themselves unable to care for themselves—it is a noble and Christian calling for anyone to help the destitute. But the vast majority of Americans find work and succeed in providing for themselves and for those they love—they don't need government hand-outs. Their success allows them to live freely without any dependence on Government, and most are very generous towards those who need help.

Currently, there is a great misperception caused by those who have seen the power of government to help the needy.

They have foolishly concluded that the government is the answer to every need faced by every American. The last thing most Americans want is the expansion of governmental power to make us all dependent on government programs. Just because there are a few people who are destitute and in need, doesn't mean the majority need the government's intervention. Most Americans find a way to make a living and support their families. What they don't want is the government coming in and taking their freedom away and taking large portions of their income through various layers of taxation and government withholdings.

This book is about core American values that developed from our humble Christian beginnings. I will mention briefly the people who influenced me the most, and you need to know they raised me to love God, love family, and love the freedom we have had in the United States. I share De Tocqueville's view that America, from her beginnings, has become great because she has been good. When we stop becoming good, we will find ourselves in decline, which is where we find ourselves at the time of the writing of this book. My call is for leaders of strong moral courage to return us to our Christian foundation and to goodness—greatness will follow.

My father, Paul Ford Davis, was born in 1923. His parents were devout Christians and schoolteachers, and his father served in the U.S. Army in World War I. If you do the math, my father was about 18 when Pearl Harbor was attacked. He joined the U.S. Marines, was trained in Marine Corps aviation as a tail gunner on the SBD Dauntless Dive Bomber, and served in the Pacific until the end of WWII. After the war, he returned to his home state, went to the University of Kentucky, completed his degree, and was working as a basketball coach and public school principal in Kentucky when he met my mother, who is also a University of Kentucky graduate. She too was raised to love God and country by her parents. Her father was a successful cattleman who owned several farms and businesses in southern Kentucky. Her degree from the University of Kentucky came about 5 years after Dad earned his degree, and was in Home Economics. She was working for Kentucky Utilities when she met my father, and they were married about a year later.

Several years after getting a doctorate my father accepted a position at Morehead State University in eastern Kentucky. I attended grades k-12 at University Breckinridge School on the campus of MSU, so I grew up in the little college town of Morehead, Kentucky. The population of the town when I was there was about 7000 people, and when the MSU students were on campus another 7000 people were added to the community.

I was raised to love God, family, and country. In high school, I determined that it would be wrong for me not to serve my country in the military. From the beginning of our nation's history to the present, we have secured our freedom through those willing to fight for it. If we ever reach a point where people are unwilling to fight to defend freedom, we will lose it. Not knowing if I could be accepted, I applied for the three service academies of our three main military branches and to other military service opportunities. Through many months of prayer and with a high interest in aviation I received a nomination and appointment to the Air Force Academy.

My parents trained me to trust in God, work hard, and respect those in authority over me. This training served me well at USAFA. My major was in international affairs. I fenced Sabre on the intercollegiate fencing team and completed Army Airborne school during my junior summer as a USAFA cadet. While my eyes did not allow me to go to pilot training, upon graduation I was given my first choice on my "dream sheet" to serve on an aircrew as a weapons director, providing target information to fighter aircraft. I served in the Air Force's Tactical Air Command under President Reagan, and my work included intercepting Soviet aircraft testing our North American defense system, flying surveillance and interdiction missions to catch drug runners at our southern border, maintaining 24-hour airborne surveillance in the mid-east during the Iran-Iraq war, and directing aircraft in full-scale battle exercises in Korea and with NATO forces at Nellis AFB, NV.

During my active-duty time, I was also asked to serve as a weapons director instructor, followed by an assignment in the Wing's command section. As Wing Executive Officer I supported the Wing Commander on a team leading the worldwide operational deployment of our E-3 "Sentry" early warning and control aircraft. As a staff officer, I began attending law school at night. After my active-duty time, I had an opportunity to transfer to a USAF Reserve unit that was upgrading from F-4s to F-16 fighter aircraft. This work allowed me to complete my law degree at night. After my time in the F-16 unit, I had the opportunity to work for the Air Force Academy in their admissions process. My work in the Air Force Reserve allowed me to practice law in private, general practice, and work as a youth and family minister. I retired after serving in the USAF in both active duty and reserve forces as a Lieutenant Colonel.

What I want you to know is that I love this country because I love freedom. Those who have served and given their lives to defend this nation have been willing to fight so we can live in a free country where we are not controlled by government tyrants. History has shown a clear pattern of government leaders who take power and become consumed with the control of their people so they can maintain power and push their self-serving agendas. These tyrannical rulers are finding their way into American public service.

The basis of the U.S. experiment, as embodied in our U.S. Constitution, is a system designed to prevent tyranny. We are to be ruled by laws passed by elected legislative bodies. Those laws are to be carried out by the executive branch, but if the executive branch is not honoring the Constitution and properly executing the laws as they are written, the Congress must hold them accountable and correct them through oversight, budgeting, and impeachment. All laws, legislative conduct, and executive conduct are ultimately under the review of the Supreme Court, which is to interpret the Constitution and our laws and rule on disputes that may arise between and within the other branches, between states, and between individuals. If any one of these three branches is not doing their job in accordance with the Constitution, the system that was designed to protect us from tyranny does not work.

There are good leaders and bad leaders in public service. During my time in military service, I served under many leaders who had strong moral courage, as demonstrated by their willingness to put their lives on the line to fight for freedom—freedom that is at the heart of what America is all about. As this book is being completed in 2024, America finds herself with a shortage of strong moral leadership— including compromised leaders in the Department of Defense, many of whom are more concerned with social experimentation and political agendas than protecting our nation from our enemies. Throughout our U.S. government, we currently have unchecked tyranny with top leaders who would rather ignore the Constitution for selfish gain than honor it.

To find a leader who demonstrated strong moral leadership, this book will frequently look to the example of Abraham Lincoln. Lincoln ultimately took a stance against slavery because it was the right moral position, not because it was politically popular. Half the country hated his position so much that they went to war to keep people in slavery. Lincoln took a stand for freedom and goodness, his enemies took a stand for slavery and evil. More on this in the next chapter, but this book will champion strong moral leadership and Lincoln will be a frequent example of what a strong moral leader does. Lincoln was not perfect, no human being is, but he knew how to take a stand for what was right.

You must be warned that the positions taken in this book on the border, on the budget, and on abortion, and the role of women in the military, to name a few, are not from the position of a politician pursuing an acceptable compromise. There are times when statesmanship and diplomacy are needed to move the ball down the field. But what is seriously missing in families, in education, in business, in media, and in the U.S. government are leaders with strong moral leadership, willing to take a stand to lead people away from what is destructive and evil, and toward what is helpful and good.

Chapter 1: Lincoln's Strong Moral Leadership

> *"I am here. I must do the best I can, and bear the responsibility of taking the course which I feel I ought to take."*[1] *Abraham Lincoln upon his announcement that he would publish his (preliminary) Emancipation Proclamation to free the slaves, during the Civil War, Sept. 22, 1862.*

For years before he was elected President of the United States, Abraham Lincoln was actively making the case against slavery. His debates on the slavery question were legendary. Stephen Douglas was arguing for the rights of U.S. citizens to own other human beings and that it should be up to each state to determine whether they would be a slave state or a free state. As shocking as it is for us to go back in history, half of the country was so focused on the rights of the slave owners to own slaves that they refused to consider the position of the slaves. Geographically, these people were predominantly in the southern states where slaves were used on big plantations owned by very wealthy landowners. When Lincoln was first elected President in 1860, the country was so divided that pro-slavery states began succeeding from the United States, and the country ended up in a civil war over a question of freedom that should have been decided decades before by reasonable lawmakers in Congress. We lacked such honorable leaders in Congress, but we found such a leader in Lincoln.

As I write this book in 2023 and 2024 the United States continues to be bitterly, radically, dangerously divided. We can only hope that we can rely on our Constitution, the Congress, and the rule of law to resolve our differences, but the differences are stark.

One side takes such positions that the border security laws should not be followed; that the government should be larger; that children should be able to decide for themselves if they want to go through sex change operations that will remove healthy sexual and reproductive body parts, and that will prevent them from having children naturally; that babies in the womb are not human enough to have the right to life; that taxpayers should pay for abortions and transgender (elective) surgeries; that when radical Palestinian Islamic extremists torture, burn alive, rape, cook babies in ovens before their parents eyes, kill over 1000 Israelis and Americans, and kidnap over 100 Israelis and Americans, that America should take the side of the Palestinians that put HAMAS terrorists into governmental power; that the United States should actively give aid to Iran and allow Iran to make millions upon millions of dollars exporting oil so Iran can support radical Islamic extremist terrorists like HAMAS and Hezbollah; that we should do away with gas engines and our oil industry in support of electric cars and trucks to save the planet from "climate change"; that we should defund the police; that we should require elementary school children to be indoctrinated by Drag Queen Story Hour programs and other pornographic materials in our public schools; that U.S. executive branch agencies should be controlled by those who want the government to control our energy companies, our health care system, and our education system; and that the government should intervene and help determine what people hear and don't hear in the media about these and other controversial policy matters.

The other side takes such positions that people should only cross U.S. borders when they come in legally; that it is primarily the responsibility of each person in the country to work to provide for their own (and their family's) food, housing, and healthcare; that children should not be allowed to have sex change operations that cut off healthy sexual body parts and that permanently harm and often make sterile their developing bodies; that babies in the womb are human beings that have the Constitutional right to life; that taxpayers should not be paying for the killing of innocent children (abortions) and for transgender (elective) surgeries; that when radical Palestinian Islamic extremists torture, burn alive, rape, cook babies in ovens before their parents eyes, kill over 1000 Israelis and Americans, and kidnap over 100 Israelis and Americans, that America should take the same position that it took in World War II against such genocidal murderers, and should be on the side of Israel to help them defeat Palestinian and Iranian extremism just as America helped defeat Germany in World War II; that the United States should not actively give aid to Iran and the U.S. should enforce sanctions to prevent Iran from making millions upon millions of dollars exporting oil, allowing them to support radical Islamic extremist terrorists like HAMAS and Hezbollah; that U.S. lawmakers should restore a thriving oil and gas industry to assure U.S. energy independence and end the U.S. government's active manipulation of the car and transportation industry and allow consumers to choose whether they want gas or electric cars and trucks; that cities should actively fund our law enforcement agencies so they are quality enforcers of the law and so they are successful crime-fighters; that we should keep Drag Queen Story Hour and other pornographic materials out of our public schools; that U.S. executive branch agencies should not be controlling our energy companies, our health care system, and our education system; and that the government should not determine what people hear and don't hear in the media about these and other controversial policy matters.

The two major groups that are divided are also divided again geographically. The first group described above is found primarily in large urban populations, while the second group described above is found primarily in smaller cities and towns, and in more rural areas. More importantly, the division also involves the media sources these two groups rely upon. Those in the urban areas tend to rely more on the major media sources that control television and the internet, while those in more rural areas are relying primarily on conservative Christian sources on the radio and media. This division is a direct result of the tyranny of the mind Thomas Jefferson warns us about in his words found at the top of his monument in Washington: "I have sworn upon the altar of God eternal hostility against every form of tyranny over the mind of man." This tyranny of the mind is currently fueled by major media sources that insidiously twist, manipulate, and misinform the public away from the truth. There are those in power who are determined to control the thoughts and minds of the public, keep them away from the truth, and tell them only what they want them to hear. We are divided between those whose minds have been controlled by information given to them by those in power in mass-media, big corporations, education, and government and those who are getting their information from sources that are independent of these mass-media and government-controlled sources of information.

Since the beginning of our nation, there have been opposing sides. There were those who wanted to stay under the tyrannical rule, but protection, of a British monarch, and there were patriots who wanted freedom and a representative form of government. Those who took the side of freedom fought and secured a country determined to be free from a tyrant's rule. As the founders began constructing a government, political conflict was frequent. The writers of the U.S. Constitution took different sides over how much power the federal government should have. The majority decided the federal government should have limited powers. This conflict continues as the federal government has taken on enormous powers, far beyond the intent of the framers.

There were opposing sides in Abraham Lincoln's day. Half of the country wanted slavery, and the other half wanted freedom for all people. For decades before the Civil War, there were those who wanted compromise, for freedom to be allowed in some states but not in others. There were also those, like Lincoln, who did not believe in compromise on such moral matters but believed that there was a right way and a wrong way and that America should take a stand and unite behind what was right and good and moral—that all people should be free. History has shown that those who fought for slavery were fighting for selfish gain, rather than for what was morally right.

What can be called "the fallacy of the Civil War South," is found in the obsession on one side of the argument that blinded them to the truth found on the other side of the argument. People in the South were so determined to fight for the rights of the slave owners via state's rights arguments that they failed to see that on the other side of the argument was immoral slavery of human beings. They were so consumed with their self-serving pro-slaveowner positions that they disgracefully missed the bigger moral issue—that it is wrong to own another person as if they are a piece of property. Those who fought for slavery for all eternity bear the shame of fighting and killing others for their own selfish greed. In disgrace, they are known in history as those responsible for a war that took the lives of over 600,000 Americans over a dispute that should have been settled in Congress where reasonable lawmakers should have agreed that slavery is immoral. This fallacy, obsessing over one's position without full and honest consideration of the other side, continues in every topic currently dividing our nation.

How important it was to have a leader like Abraham Lincoln who saw clearly the moral question, and was determined to not compromise, even in a time of great division. Confederate leaders who left the union were not only blinded by their obsession with the rights of slave owners, but they were also being guided by pragmatism rather than principle. It was more practical and convenient for them to continue in an economy that exploited slave labor than to go through the difficult process of freeing the slaves and building an economy on paid labor. This high level of pragmatism continues to be a major problem as many Americans prefer convenience, for example of using corrupt social media companies, rather than acting on principle, and moving to another social media source. The practical usefulness of a popular social media platform rules the habits of a majority of Americans. In this pragmatism, there is a disregard for the company owners who use their billions to advance their immoral positions.

As long as we have freedom, we will have opposing sides. Leaders are needed like Lincoln who will not be blinded by the fallacy of seeing only one side of a question while missing the moral question clearly seen on the other side.

We need leaders who will stand on principles even when it is inconvenient or not practical. History will continue to reveal those who make good choices to stand for what is right, and those who make bad choices to stand for what is evil.

Lincoln had the moral courage to do what was right, even when it was difficult. We also call this integrity. The application of integrity to national problems can resolve differences and unify the nation. For this to happen we need leaders with integrity to stand for truth and the rule of law as found in the Constitution and in the laws passed by Congress. The alternative is for us to have bad leaders who are more concerned with selfish power and the taking away of life and liberty rather than protecting life and preserving the freedom paid for by the blood of our patriots. Many still also do not understand the clear role of law—that freedom does not include the freedom of a person to pursue selfish gain that harms another person. We need leaders with integrity, that seek truth not lies, who seek what is good not what is evil, and who understand government's limited role. But can we find leaders with the moral courage to honor these truths?

Chapter 2: Integrity First

"In giving freedom to the slave, we assure freedom to the free—honorable alike in what we give and what we preserve."[2] Abraham Lincoln

When I first served in the U.S. Air Force in the 1980s, we had three core values: integrity first, service before self, and excellence in all we do. Our clear mission was to be the strongest Air Force on the planet as part of the strongest military on the planet, so no other country would dare go against us. It was called peace through strength.

Integrity was first because if you have integrity, and you are given a job to fix an airplane, operate an airplane, fix a weapon, operate a weapon, attack a target, destroy a target, or do any associated work in support of military aviation, you must honestly do your job. As a mechanic you fix the equipment you are tasked to repair, and when you sign off the maintenance books you are affirming that you have done your job to make the weapons system operational in accordance with the technical orders governing that weapon's system. If you are in operations and you are given the task to complete your part of a battle plan, it is your duty to accomplish your assigned task per the air order you are given.

Integrity is first, because lives are at stake, the operational mission is at stake, and our nation's defense is at stake. If there is a breach of integrity, airplanes may crash, weapons may fail, and tragic loss of life may result. These failures not only can deny success in a current battle, but breaches of integrity must be corrected or there will be continued failures and a lack of trust between those involved, and ultimately the failure of the military to accomplish its mission.

Like the USAF, each federal government agency has the responsibility to honor the laws from Congress that define their work. The principle of integrity applied to our executive branch agencies can be defined as being honest and faithfully executing U.S. laws. There must be honesty and openness about current challenges. If executive branch agencies are not faithfully completing their lawful work assignments, or if there is unlawful conduct coming from executive branch leadership, this conduct must be corrected, and those responsible held accountable by Congress. Integrity requires the executive branch to faithfully execute the laws passed through Congress, and integrity requires Congress to correct the executive branch for failure to faithfully execute their duties.

If senior executive branch leaders commit treason, bribery, or other high crimes dangerous to our nation, the United States House of Representatives should do their job and impeach them and send such cases to the Senate for trial. This is not about politics. This is not about being a member of a certain political party. This is not about a fear of a pattern of political retribution. This is about having the integrity to do the right thing—if dangerous criminals are in positions of power in the executive branch, they should be removed from office by impeachment.

If the U.S. House of Representatives sends articles of impeachment to the U.S. Senate, the Senate should then do their job and conduct a trial to bring the facts and evidence to the Senate's members and in so doing to the American people. This is not a matter of accepting or denying the case—the Constitution requires that the Senate conduct the trial. If the Senate fails to do its job to take the Impeachment to trial, the House should bring a Petition (file a legal action) to require the Senate to do its job. And if the Senate refuses to follow the Constitution the House should appeal the case to the Supreme Court to demand the Senate follow the Constitution. No matter their party, if the evidence shows that top U.S. executive branch leaders have committed impeachable crimes dangerous to our nation, Senators with integrity should vote for impeachment.

It is often argued that impeachment is a waste of time when one, or both, branches of Congress do not have the political majority to advance the impeachment process. But this should not be a matter of pragmatism or politics. This should be a matter of integrity. If the facts show that senior executive branch leaders are not faithfully executing their duties, or are committing treason, bribery, or other high crimes, members of Congress, no matter what their political party may be, should do their duty and faithfully advance the prosecution of impeachment.

In impeachment, Congress is in the role of a prosecutor. If there are dangerous crimes being committed in any community, including the executive branch of government, they should be prosecuted. In our local communities, especially in small and mid-sized towns, citizens of those towns generally do not tolerate crime problems. Elected officials should prosecute crime and keep communities safe, or they will not be in office for very long because, in most U.S. towns and cities, local citizens will vote them out of office.

Voters should hold accountable each member of Congress for their willingness to prosecute or ignore treason, bribery, or other high crimes committed by senior executive branch leaders, including the President of the

United States. Though currently rare, if given the opportunity members of Congress may surprise us and vote with integrity, based on facts and laws, rather than casting their vote based on blind allegiance to their political party. We desperately need members of Congress with the integrity to honor the facts and the law, and if dangerous criminal behavior is found with senior executive branch leaders, those leaders should be removed from office by impeachment. Otherwise, our system of government does not work, and we are left with dangerous executive branch leaders in power.

What we need today in America are leaders who have the integrity and the courage to do what is right—even in the face of fierce opposition. Too many current leaders in Congress and the U.S. federal government are unwilling to do what is right either because of political reasons or because it is too difficult. Being honest and doing what is right is usually not practical, it's generally not easy. Lincoln understood this well.

Most of us have great appreciation for Abraham Lincoln's leadership in standing for freedom in the U.S. Civil War. But do we truly comprehend how divisive his stance was when he was elected President in 1860? History records how difficult it was for him to stand for what was right. He was hated by those who were for slavery and faced constant death threats and a horrific war that took the lives of over 600,000 Americans. Ultimately, he was killed because of his willingness to lead based on principle, not pragmatism.

Having integrity is not for the faint of heart. Lincoln knew this and knew that if you stand on principle for what is wise and true and moral and good you will have supporters, but you will also have many who will oppose you. We look back now and view Lincoln's enemies as foolish, misinformed, and missing the moral principle that slavery is wrong. Lincoln's enemies included half of the country and they were so opposed to him that they took arms against him en masse. But this did not deter him from doing the right thing—leading United States forces in the defense of freedom for all people.

It should be acknowledged that Lincoln's strength to stand for what was right was based on his humble faith in God. Lincoln did not rely on his own wisdom or strength, but he knew with great clarity that our fundamental rights as human beings come from God. As we read in our Declaration of Independence:

"We hold these truths to be self-evident, that all men (people) are created equal, that they are endowed by their Creator with certain unalienable Rights, that among these are Life, Liberty, and the pursuit of Happiness.

That to secure these rights, Governments are instituted among Men, deriving their just powers from the consent of the governed."

Our fundamental rights to life, liberty, and the pursuit of happiness, come from God, and they are secured through government with the consent of the people. Trust in the God-honoring principles of honesty and integrity drives the answers given in this book to our nation's problems. To each problem America is facing with the U.S. federal government the principles associated with integrity are applied. These principles of honesty and doing what is right are first and foremost from the wisdom of God—the same God that Lincoln often acknowledged in his strong stand for freedom.

Are we on the verge of another Civil War? Even though we live in a country that is divided, it is my position that most Americans today are willing for our political process to resolve our differences. There are extremists on both sides that may be militant and willing to violently promote their cause, but most Americans, including this author, think we are in a time when we should be able to have open debate, arguments made through a free press, elections, lawmaking in legislative bodies, and use of the court system to resolve our differences. Americans need to elect leaders willing to stand for what is right, demanding honesty and integrity as we work to resolve our differences, using the systems found in the U.S. Constitution.

Whether we are talking about border security, the national budget, the military, terrorists, the Department of Justice, elections, Congress, freedom of religion, freedom of speech, freedom of the press, freedom to assemble, racism, corporate America, mass media, defining what a man is or what a woman is, marriage and family, a baby's right to life, children's rights, parents' rights, education, healthcare, men competing in women's sports, women in combat, or any other topic where we have differences of opinion in the United States; if we could simply be honest with the facts, and have the integrity to do what is right and lawful, we could resolve every problem.

Don't believe me? Seems too simple? In the following chapters the application of "Integrity First" is shown as a solution to problem after problem. Each topic will be addressed by first giving an "intelligence briefing." Before flying an operational mission for the Air Force, we always received an intelligence briefing. This briefing from an intelligence officer provided us with the facts on the threats we faced that day. For example, the briefings included current information on where enemy military weapons systems were located that could be a threat to us. It was critical that those giving us these briefings had the integrity to give us the facts about the mission ahead and the threats we faced, and that we had the integrity to meet the threats and do the jobs we were assigned.

The chapters that follow each begin with an "Intelligence Brief" section which reviews the facts associated with a current problem or policy. One of the major causes of the great divide in our nation is that news and media sources lack the integrity to report facts objectively and accurately. Depending on where you get your news, your view of the facts may be very different from what is revealed in this book. Sources listed vary, and where you may be in disbelief of facts presented you are encouraged to do your own research. It is critical that we seek and find truth on any topic with honesty and integrity. Truth cannot be found if we only hear from sources that tickle our ears and share our own biases. Facts must be sought from both sides of any question. It is understood that facts involved on any topic selected may be constantly developing, but where truth is found integrity can then be applied to provide solutions to difficult problems.

After the Intelligence Brief section, the "Integrity First Answer" section of every chapter follows. This section outlines the work that should be accomplished to help resolve the problem. It must be acknowledged that this book is not the trier of fact and law in cases where leaders may have behaved unlawfully. The press is not the trier of fact. Book authors are not the triers of fact. In the United States of America, we honor the rule of law. Disputes of fact and law are resolved through legal processes. As we seek solutions to our problems, we will find questions that should be addressed through the U.S. legal system, where there is due process and where justice can be officially obtained. As to federal questions of executive branch conduct, this legal system includes the duty of the Congress to oversee and correct criminal activity found in the executive branch.

The Integrity First Answer sections identify the proper legal process that should be followed to apply the facts to the law in disputed matters. These sections identify who is responsible for correcting unlawful conduct from government officials, and the process that should be followed. These processes may seem like mountains too high to climb. Any lawyer knows some problems are large and complex. America needs elected leaders with integrity who are willing to honestly do their jobs, even though their work may be very difficult and time-consuming.

Integrity first answers are not about making decisions in accordance with the marching orders of a certain political party. Integrity first is about doing what is honest, and doing what is right, instead of blindly following political party agendas. This is the leadership of Lincoln—in a time of great division, taking the side of truth and integrity, and uniting America in what is morally good and right.

History has shown very clearly that there was a right side and a wrong side in the U.S. Civil War. Those living in that divided nation were living in a time when they had to make a choice—which side would they be on? It was not a time for compromise. Those who had the integrity to fight for the freedom of the slaves were on the right side. Those who fought for the rights of the slave owners were on the wrong side.

Numerous topics on which our nation is divided are covered in the following chapters. It is again time to choose which side we are on. This is not a time to stand in the middle. History will clearly show whether we are on the right side or the wrong side. On which side will you be?

Chapter 3: The Border and Immigration

"In times like the present, men should utter nothing for which they would not willingly be responsible through time and eternity."[3] Abraham Lincoln, during the bitter war between the North and the South.

Intelligence Brief: The State of the Border

Many American citizens travel actively to other nations and in their travels, they honor the country that they are visiting. They bring their passports, follow the laws of any foreign nation they enter, and bring any paperwork required by that foreign nation for lawful entry. We understand that each country has its own laws for the security and safety of its own people.

The United States should be no different than other modern nations. Congress has passed laws defining the process to enter the United States legally. These laws are designed to protect our nation from those who could do us harm. Like any law that is passed to protect us, if it is not enforced there are those who will ignore it. As with speed limit laws, if they are not enforced on a section of the highway there are people who will dangerously ignore the law and speed. If our border laws are not enforced there are people who will come to the United States who will ignore our laws—and the very dangers to Americans that our laws seek to prevent become realities for the American people.

Border security laws have been passed to protect Americans from terrorists. If we don't know who is coming across the border we allow people to come here who are actively planning to commit terrorist attacks in the United States. We know firsthand from 9-11-2001 and other terrorist incidents that there are people out there determined to conduct terrorist attacks against unsuspecting Americans. The head of the Border Patrol in 2021, Rodney Scott, said in August of 2021, "I firmly believe that it is a national security crisis. Immigration is just a subcomponent of it, and right now, it's just a cover for massive amounts of smuggling going across the southwest border—to include TSDBs (known or suspected terrorists) at a level we have never seen before. That's a real threat."[4] This failure to enforce our laws opens the door to terrorists to commit future attacks and only helps our enemies enter the United States undetected. National executive branch leaders willfully failing to stop terrorists at our borders makes those executive branch leaders supporters of terrorism. This is "aiding and abetting" the enemies of the United States, and according to the U.S. Constitution, this is treason.[5]

Sex trafficking is a high crime and because of our lack of enforcement of immigration laws, our senior federal government leadership is acting as a partner in the life-destroying crime of enslaving children. As described in one report, children are turned over to "sponsors" who enslave them when "….smugglers persuade parents to hand over their children in pursuit of a 'better life,' taking advantage of policies that virtually guarantee the release of the unaccompanied minor to a sponsor in the United States. In 2022, nearly 130,000 such minors were released to a sponsor, a new record."[6] We know this unlawful child abuse is going on. Laws are in place for legal immigration, passed by Congress, to prevent this. The willful failure of our senior leadership to simply do their job to ensure immigration laws are enforced has resulted in a constant increase in the abuse and destruction of the lives of children enslaved in sex-trafficking. This willful and reckless failure to enforce our immigration laws makes our senior executive branch leaders complicit in this horrific high crime of sex-trafficking.

Because of non-enforcement of border laws senior U.S. leaders are aiding and abetting the drug cartels, gangs, and other drug traffickers who are bringing dangerous drugs, like fentanyl, into the U.S. in record amounts. Deaths from Fentanyl and other illegal drugs have been radically increasing over the last several years.[7] The willful failure to enforce immigration laws makes those U.S. senior executive leaders responsible for enforcing these laws participants in the reckless killing of thousands of Americans. It is well known that Fentanyl and other dangerous drugs are now more lethal than ever before. This is why Congress has passed laws requiring anyone coming to the United States to do so with legal review to prevent dangerous illegal drugs from pouring into our country. In the failure to enforce our nation's immigration laws the U.S. executive branch leaders are guilty of allowing large quantities of these dangerous drugs to come across our borders, and are therefore guilty of the high crimes of drug-trafficking and reckless homicide that unavoidably result from the availability of these dangerous drugs.

Also heartbreaking are the numerous cases of illegal aliens who commit crimes against American citizens. Every time an American is the victim of a crime done by someone who was allowed to come into the United States Illegally, whether the crime is stealing, rape, murder, or any other criminal act, the U.S. government is to blame for allowing that individual into the country without proper review.

The millions of people crossing the U.S. border illegally from 2021 to 2024 are the equivalent of an invasion of foreign nationals, many of whom are from countries like China that we know threaten our own country. Since President Biden took over in January of 2021 more than 3.8 million illegal aliens have been allowed to enter our country—a number higher than the population of at least 22 or our current states.[8] A large number of these illegal immigrants are young men of military age who could be part of future plans to destroy our nation from the inside. We do not know the full extent of all the dangers that could be involved because we are not enforcing the laws to allow *legal immigration-* words you seldom hear or see written in the press.

We do know that those who are coming into the U.S. illegally do not have respect for our laws—they are law-breakers by just being in our country and ignoring our laws. Those actually seeking asylum may be the exceptions, and many children have been brought into the United States at the mercy of their law-breaking guardians or captors, but the dangers of the massive numbers of those who have entered our borders illegally are real and are treasonous. When the United States is not enforcing our immigration laws at the border the federal government is unquestionably aiding our enemies by allowing a number of foreign nationals into the U.S. who are not honoring U.S. laws but whose citizenship is in countries known to be dangerous to the U.S.

While this book was being written HAMAS terrorists horrifically attacked innocent civilian families in Israel, killing, raping, and torturing innocent men, women, and children. This is what happens when borders are overrun by terrorists. Border patrol has reported a "spike in encounters between agents and terror watchlist suspects attempting to enter the U.S. illegally and undetected at the southern border in fiscal year 2023."[9] What about terrorists that are not on the watchlist? Do we honestly think the only terrorists out there are the ones on the terrorist watchlist? What about all the new terrorists and the unknown terrorists that are not on the list? By not properly vetting each person crossing the U.S. borders, not only are we missing terrorists coming into our nation that may be on a terrorist watchlist, but without enforcing our border laws we have no idea how many terrorists are coming into America that are not on the watchlists. This is why we must have border security and this is why we must individually review every case to make sure everyone coming into our country is following our laws and not here to hurt us.

Integrity First Answer: Congress Should Impeach Senior Leaders Guilty of Treason and High Crimes for Not Enforcing Border and Immigration Laws

The Integrity First Answer starts at the top of the executive branch with the President, Vice President and senior staff who have committed to faithfully honor the U.S. Constitution and execute the laws of Congress. The oath taken by each U.S. President, per Article II, Section 1, of the U.S. Constitution includes, "I will faithfully execute the Office of the President of the United States." This is repeated in Article II, Section 3, where it states the

President, "shall take Care that the Laws be faithfully executed…"

From Marbury v. Madison, 5 U.S. 137 (1803), to other similar cases, the U.S. Supreme Court has affirmed the importance of the separation of powers, and that it is the duty of the President to faithfully execute the nation's laws in accordance with the Constitution, whether he agrees with them or not.[10] For example, from Kendall v. United States ex Rel. Stokes, 37 U.S. 524 (1838), where the Court ruled it could not sanction executive power in opposition to the laws of Congress, it is stated: "It would be vesting in the President a dispensing power which has no countenance for its support in any part of the Constitution, and is asserting a principle which, if carried out in its results to all cases falling within it, would be clothing the President with a power entirely to control the legislation of Congress and paralyze the administration of Justice."[11]

Much of our border debate comes down to this question of who makes the laws in the United States? Is it the Congress, who has passed laws on legal immigration? Or does the President and his executive branch make the laws? What most Americans know, and what was affirmed in the Kendall case just quoted, is that it is very dangerous for the President to take over law-making power, as law-making is the job of Congress. One government official making laws is tyranny. The job of the executive branch is to execute and enforce the laws passed by Congress. When the executive branch fails to do this but instead allows millions of people to come into the U.S. in violation of laws passed by Congress, has not the President and his executive branch taken the power of rule-making and come up with their own laws?

The President's duty is to faithfully execute the laws, including immigration laws, and his failure to execute these laws is a breach of his constitutional duty. The only way to correct this unlawful behavior is through impeachment. As stated in the Kendall case: "The executive power is vested in a President, and as far as his powers are derived from the Constitution, he is beyond the reach of any other department except in the mode prescribed by the Constitution through the impeachment power."[12]

Integrity demands that we be honest about the executive branch's failure to enforce U.S. immigration laws. People should only be allowed into the United States if they come in legally. The Integrity First Answer demands that our laws be enforced. The executive branch should do the job they have been given to protect our border. Millions have been allowed into the country without honoring U.S. immigration laws, and, per the above Intelligence Brief, the lack of enforcement of our nation's laws has assisted our enemies and is therefore treasonous, and is evidence of other high crimes to include, child trafficking, drug trafficking, and reckless homicide.

The U.S. Congress is given impeachment powers for the dismissal from public office of our top executive leaders for failure to faithfully execute their duties, for treason, or for other high crimes. If the top three top executive branch leaders, the President, the Vice President, and the Secretary of Homeland Security, are letting millions of people into the United States illegally, they are clearly responsible for this treasonous and criminal behavior.

When multiple criminals are guilty of dangerous crimes in any jurisdiction, city, county, state, or federal, those in prosecutor roles should do their duty and enforce the laws, no matter how many are committing crimes. When there is more than one senior leader in our executive branch committing dangerous crimes the Congress is not limited to one impeachment, but the facts and the law may dictate that several top executive branch leaders be impeached for their crimes.

In our federal executive branch, if the U.S. President is committing treason for failure to enforce immigration laws aiding our enemies by giving them free access to America, Congress has a duty to impeach the President and remove him or her from office. In the United States, the Vice President was given the responsibility for securing our border during the Biden Administration.[13] If that Vice President failed to secure the border, and committed treason by assisting our enemies in giving them free access to our country, that Vice President should have been impeached by the Congress and removed from office for treason and other related high crimes. If the Secretary of the U.S. Department of Homeland Security, who according to U.S. law is responsible for securing the border, was not enforcing U.S. law and was allowing people to enter the U.S. border illegally, that Secretary should also have been impeached by Congress for treason and high crimes for allowing our enemies free access to our country. Thank God for Congressman Mark Green, who actually was a leader with moral courage that got this impeachment work done and delivered the case to the Senate—then the Senate violated the Constitution by not trying the case (more on this in the next few paragraphs). The U.S. House of Representatives is in the role of the prosecutor, and they should file impeachment articles for all top senior officials who are failing to faithfully execute U.S. immigration laws, for committing treason by aiding our enemies by giving them free access to America, and for committing other high crimes.

As with any prosecutor, city, county, state, or federal, facts and law should determine what cases are filed and who is charged. Dangerous criminals should be prosecuted for their crimes. When prosecutors do their jobs, they file their cases, present the facts and the law, and then rely on the jury to make the right decision, based on the evidence and the laws that have been violated. It is wrong to not bring a case to a jury just because of a lack of trust in the jury. Prosecutors must have the courage to enforce the laws, and then leave it to the strength of the law and the facts, presented to the jury, to convict criminals. Prosecutors without moral courage use their prosecutorial discretion to not enforce laws that are against their political agendas, and they immorally prosecute laws and misuse the laws to attack and imprison their political enemies.

For impeachment, once the U.S. House approves articles of impeachment, the Senate is then required to conduct the trial. It would be a breach of integrity to fail to file valid Articles of Impeachment based solely on a political judgment that the Senate will not do its job to decide a case based on the facts and the law. If the facts show impeachable offenses, the House has the duty to produce Articles of Impeachment, and the Senate has the duty to conduct the trial. If the Senate refuses to bring the case to trial the House should bring a legal action against the Senate to compel the Senate to follow the Constitution and do their job. This way the facts and law can clearly be produced for all to see, and members of the Senate, acting as the jury, can be accountable for all of history to judge, whether the facts and the laws justify impeachment. If the facts clearly show impeachable conduct, and if Senators have integrity, they should vote to impeach.

What should be done with the millions who are now in the United States illegally? The Integrity First Answer is for the executive branch to enforce the laws passed by Congress. Those who have entered illegally, and have cut line ahead of the thousands who are honoring our immigration laws, should face the legal deportation process. If they don't have a legal reason to be here (which could include asylum or if they are children who need protection from abuse) they should be returned to their place of unlawful entry, or to the location required for deportation in accordance with U.S. laws.

As an attorney, I have worked with deportation proceedings, and in most cases, due process can be given with a single hearing that allows each case to be considered individually. If it is confirmed the illegal immigrant has not honored our immigration laws they can be deported out of the United States. The deportation process allows for more attention to be given to valid cases of asylum, or to the unique concerns that come from protecting minors. Each deportation case is unique and each person should be given due process, but the majority of the illegal aliens that are in the United States have simply come in without following U.S. immigration laws and they should not be allowed to stay when their presence is a continuing violation of laws passed by Congress.

There is no integrity in shipping illegal aliens all over the U.S. and paying them and housing them for their crimes. Those here illegally should be given their day in court in accordance with the deportation process, and if they are here illegally they should be deported. In other words, instead of being given a free ticket, with room and board to travel to cities all over America, they should be given a ticket back across the border. If they are here illegally and if they have integrity, they should leave the U.S. of their own accord. If they want to come to the United States, they should honor our laws, not insult us by disregarding them. If we ended all the financial support we are giving to those coming across our border illegally many may be more willing to leave on their own. The duty of government officials is to enforce our laws, not enable law-breakers.

Many will say that deporting those who are here illegally is too big a job, it is unrealistic, it is impossible. Living with integrity means doing the right thing, even when it is very difficult. Yes, it will be difficult to enforce U.S. immigration laws. It's difficult to enforce our murder laws, and our drug trafficking laws, and our sex trafficking laws—it's difficult to enforce any of our laws. Congress has passed laws that pertain to immigration and United States executive branches should have the integrity and courage to enforce these laws.

This is the leadership of Lincoln—in a time of great division, taking the side of truth and integrity, leading us to unity in what is morally good and right. Do we honor and enforce our laws passed by Congress to protect our nation's border from those who would harm us, or disregard them? The integrity first answer is to honor and enforce our laws.

Chapter 4: The Federal (Non-)Budget

"The man of integrity walks securely, but he who takes crooked paths will be found out." Proverbs 10: 9

Intelligence Brief: U.S. Debt and Spending

The United States Congress continues, year after year, to recklessly spend trillions of dollars that that we do not have in revenue, thus endlessly increasing our federal government's debt. The amount of this debt is so high it is beyond the comprehension of most of us. The United States federal government owes over $34 trillion at the time of this writing in 2024—with a Republican majority in the House of Representatives and a Democrat majority in the Senate. It is clear that reckless spending by the Congress is a bipartisan sport.

Most of us have a very difficult time getting our heads around 34 trillion dollars—most of us have a hard time comprehending 1 billion dollars. Most of our homes are priced somewhere between $100,000 and $1,000,000, so we can grasp 1 million dollars. But when you move from $1 million ($1,000,000) to $100 million ($100,000,000), it gets a little more difficult. When you get to $999 million ($999,000,000.00) it gets even more difficult. So few of us can comprehend 1 billion dollars ($1,000,000,000), and fewer can truly comprehend 1000 billion which is 1 trillion dollars ($1,000,000,000,000). So with $34 trillion in debt Congress has placed more debt on Americans than most of us can even get our minds around—it is so unbelievably massive.

Another way to try to explain it would be to describe $34 trillion in terms of the debt we have per person in the United States. So if you estimate that there are about 340 million people in the United States, adults and children, sharing $34 trillion in debt, this would be about $100,000 of debt per person. And this just keeps getting greater every hour of every day.

Another way to look at our debt is in relation to our gross domestic product (GDP). There was a time when we were trying to keep our national debt below annual GDP. Our GDP in 2022 was $26.132 trillion dollars,[14] but our debt is well beyond that now, at over $34 trillion.

Needless to say, our debt is a disgrace. Most men and women in America work hard to leave large amounts of wealth to their children, not debt. Our Congress, on the other hand, is recklessly leaving a massive amount of debt to our children. Said another way, Congress has already spent massive amounts of the future production of our children's and grandchildren's labor that is needed to pay off the federal government's debt.

There is no integrity in spending, year after year, trillions of dollars that we do not have in our federal accounts. We have massive debt in our current federal estate, yet this debt is only increasing, with no plan to even start paying it down.

We are much more vulnerable to our enemies when we have so much debt, especially when we have borrowed billions from them. From the November 2022 numbers, China owned $870 billion of U.S. debt.[15] Having such massive debt is destabilizing to our economy, makes us vulnerable to our enemies, and ties up massive U.S. spending just to service the interest on our debt.

Consider the approximately $500 billion in 2022 we paid to service our national debt.[16] As with any budget, if you pay off your debt, that money that was being spent to pay interest and principal becomes available for other, more constructive purposes. If we had our debt paid off the $500 billion our nation now pays annually to service our debt would be available to actually help our nation. For example, this would mean that each state would have $10 billion for highways and other infrastructure. Can you imagine if a member of Congress came up with $10 billion in federal funding for their state's infrastructure?

Most members of Congress are very excited to report back to their constituents when they score $5 million, or $10 million, or $30 million for some local project. What we see members of Congress do over and over is push and celebrate the passing of millions of dollars in government appropriations for some current political priority, or for a local project in their state—but they don't tell you about the billions in federal spending for other spending items that were in the legislation they voted to pass in areas they and most taxpayers don't want.

In our current system, when Congress faces budget and appropriation legislation they are facing blackmail. To get the few millions of dollars they want to get approved for their state, claim victory, and assure their reelection, they must vote for billions of dollars in other federal spending on things that their voters would clearly be against if they only knew where these billions of dollars in spending were going.

For an example of what this looks like in annual numbers, consider 2022 when the United States had approximately

$4.9 trillion in revenues, but our total "outlays" were approximately $6.3 trillion. Our federal deficit, what we overspent, that is to say, the money spent that we did not have in revenues that year, was about $1.4 trillion.[17] Better said, we didn't really have $1.4 trillion or $6.3 trillion to spend because we started the year with a negative balance of over $29.6 trillion.[18] So the over spending of our Congress just keeps happening, and the debt just keeps getting higher—over $33 trillion in 2023, and over $34 trillion in 2024.

Integrity First Answer: Stop Spending More Than We Take In, Cut Spending, and Pay Off Our Debt

There is no integrity for our Congress, the ones who have the power of the purse, to continue to engage in the ongoing blackmail that is our federal budgeting system. If this level of reckless spending was going on in any other organization—a business, a school, a non-profit organization—this would be a breach of a fiduciary duty and there would be legal action to hold accountable those responsible. This lack of responsible leadership in the Congress, this lack of honesty with the voters, this breach of their fiduciary duty to every American, this ongoing spending of trillions of dollars each year that we simply do not have would be judged as criminal in our legal system. If our voters had integrity they would stop sending politicians to Congress who continue to engage in this reckless spending. The most fundamental Integrity First Answer to our budget crisis is for the Congress to cut spending immediately so that we are spending substantially less than our annual revenues, and to allow a budget that aggressively pays down our national debt.

Most Americans maintain a budget. We look at each line-item, and we budget to not spend more money each month than what we take in. Most of us also have faced times when we spend more than we have in income for a limited time, but we know that this generates a debt that integrity demands we pay back as soon as possible. When we are paying on a debt there is interest involved, and the use of future pay for past expenses. If we have integrity, we plan and budget carefully to quickly pay back any debt we have generated. As soon as possible we budget for the debt to be paid back so that any pay that had been used for interest and other service charges can be available for current budget items, such as investments and building an estate that we can leave to our family and to others in need. To review these simple budgeting practices may seem like an insult to your intelligence, but they are not being applied in our U.S. Congress.

There have been numerous laws passed by Congress requiring balanced budgets, but rarely does the Congress follow their own laws. Instead of honoring the annual budget process, and honoring laws that have been passed demanding a process that may require across the budget cuts to balance the budget, Congress usually reaches the end of a time period when prior appropriations are about to expire and new appropriations packages have not been put in place. They then use this precarious situation to pass a "Continuing Resolution," a short term spending measure, limited in time, but that maintains the status quo, and typically keeps everything funded at current levels while often adding a few additional spending items, and of course continuing the federal money pouring into their constituents. Any good that could be done by balanced budget laws that apply to the annual budget process are ignored in the Continuing Resolution process. And when these budgets are passed short or long term, members of Congress are generally pleased that there will be no cuts in the spending of the millions they want at the local levels, in a system requiring them to fund billions of dollars in federal spending they and their constituents don't want—the blackmail mentioned in the Intelligence Briefing section above.

To avoid this blackmail, the Congress should simply require the same process in any appropriations bill that most any responsible American uses in their monthly budget—this process is line-item budgeting. In other words, for any legislation that appropriates funds, short or long term, including Continuing Resolutions, each line-item of spending for a specific purpose or project should require the separate approval of each member of Congress. Each independent measure in the budget, each line-item should be given a spot for a "Yes" or a "No" vote. No more being forced to vote for federal spending on items the member of Congress doesn't want. Each item in the budget should pass or fail on its own merit. This would also require members of Congress to read and review each spending item, and would make them clearly accountable for what they support and do not support.

If the House passes a budget bill with line items that were approved by the majority of the House, and the Senate changes line items of great importance to the House, the House majority that passed the House version of the Bill should stand their ground and not pass a compromised Senate version of the bill that removed items important to the nation and to the majority of the House. If the Senate refuses to accept the items required by the House majority, and a shutdown of the government is threatened, House leaders should communicate clearly that it is the Senate that is refusing to honor what is important to the nation, and the Senate will then be under pressure to accept the House version.

Many may say that this will never happen because too many members of Congress get what they want for their local Districts and States through the current system. There is no integrity in the current system—there is blackmail, but there is not integrity, and the American people are being left with a bill that is getting harder and harder to pay each day. The Integrity First Answer is for our Congress to change the system to line-item budgeting for all appropriations legislation, including Continuing Resolutions.

Some may remember that we have had Presidents ask for line-item veto powers to give them the power to sign for items they approve in legislation passed by the Congress, but veto the items they disapprove. The U.S. Supreme Court has ruled that Presidents do not have line-item veto power, because this line-item power in our federal budget process is a power for the Congress.[19] Do not wrongfully conclude that the Supreme Court has made line-item budgeting unconstitutional for Congress—the opposite is actually true. The Supreme Court has ruled line-item voting is clearly within the power of Congress, and thus lawful for Congress. It could be said they have ruled this is the power of a responsible Congress, to consider each line-item, and pass or fail each independent item on its own merits.

Like our own personal budgets, when we generate debt our federal budgets should include funds to pay off the debt. As it is currently we just keep going deeper and deeper into debt and never get to the Integrity First Answer to start paying down the debt. With over $34 trillion in debt and approximately $5 trillion in annual federal revenue, one aggressive example of a plan to pay off our debt would be to budget $1 trillion each year to pay on the balance of the debt. Discretionary spending was $1.7 trillion in 2022, but consider the possibility of massively cutting our spending to massively cut our debt. To help with this, note that substantial federal spending cuts would be much more possible if Congress was using line-item budgeting (where members of Congress were no longer being blackmailed to approve spending they did not want).

If we paid $1 trillion on our debt each year and kept paying the interest, currently around $500 billion per year, which could decrease each year as we pay down the balance, the debt could be paid in less than 33 years. This would mean that within most of our lifetimes we could pay off our national debt and take this burden away from our children and grand-children. Making large annual payments on our debt may seem impossible. It will take us rethinking how we have been spending our money, for example, using line-item budgeting for each and every appropriations bill, including Continuing Resolutions (CR's) and debt limit increases. By making significant cuts in our federal budget we can plan to make substantial payments on the debt, with the clear goal of having the debt paid off as quickly as possible.

Another showing of weakness in our Congress is how the U.S. House of Representatives, supposedly made up of leaders who are fiscally conservative, cower to the Democrats and keep passing massive spending bills. There is such a fear of "shutting down the government" that Republicans refuse to keep a strong stance to cut the budget. The Congress is ultimately in charge of the money. The Republicans in the House could pass a budget, be it in a

CR, or other appropriations legislation, that funds the key parts of government that so many are afraid will not be funded if the government "shuts down." They could fund the military, and social security, and Medicare and Medicaid, and a few other items that should be prioritized, like parts of the DOJ. They could then not fund major amounts of other discretionary spending, keep budgeted amounts below receipts, include a substantial payment on the debt, and send this to the Senate. The Democrats in the Senate will kick and scream about additional items they want in the budget, but if the House would hold its ground, they could shift the pressure to the Senate Democrats to do the right thing and cut spending. Critical parts of the government would be funded, so the blame cannot be on the Republicans in the House for shutting down vital parts of the government, as the funding for the vital parts of the U.S. government would be in the bill. Should the Democrats in the Senate refuse to pass the bill, they would be the ones shutting down the government, not the Republicans in the House.

Another Integrity First way to accelerate the paying down of our debt is to challenge each American who has received payments from the government in their lifetimes to consider paying it back. After you pick yourself up off the floor from laughing hysterically at this idea—consider the Integrity First answer. For example, consider money we may have received during Covid or with other federal assistance programs, that may or may not have been needed at the time, but that allowed us to be in a much better position today. For those with integrity, these funds given to us by our federal government, often without our asking, that were above our income levels that did not change for most of us, could be returned in payments to the

U.S. Government. This may not be reasonable for many Americans who may have faced high tax rates, and have already overpaid the government themselves. But an integrity first answer would have us each consider money or benefits we may have received from the U.S. Government, even tax credits that resulted in the receipt of payments from the government during times of need, and consider whether or not we are in a position to pay back this money that was given to us. For administration of this return of funds, all that would be required is an additional line on our tax returns giving us the option to pay an additional amount that would go only to the national debt. Of course, the Federal Government would need to be held accountable to assure these funds were applied only to the debt.

With the application of integrity through these types of solutions to actually pay off the U.S. debt, we will be able to leave our children and grandchildren a positive and strong federal estate, one that is secure as we face our enemies, rather than one that is weak and gives an advantage to our enemies.

Integrity First answers to the budget will also require audits and special attention from the Congress to ensure the executive branch agencies are spending federal money in accordance with the measures passed by Congress. We have clearly seen that just because the Congress passes laws does not mean the executive branch will execute them. So Congress has a responsibility to be active in oversight and correction in those cases where a federal agency's leadership is failing to follow the budget given to them by Congress.

The amount of work required for Congress to honor these Integrity First approaches may also require them to work a week more in line with how most Americans work. Most Americans work 5 to 6 days a week. Congress has been averaging only about 2 days a week on federal legislative duties.[20] They should be working at least 4 or 5 days a week on their primary federal duties. In other words, to work with integrity and take the time to do their job right, their work days need to be reprioritized to work more days on their primary job as members of our U.S. Congress.

This is the leadership of Lincoln—in a time of great division, taking the side of truth and integrity, leading us to unity in what is morally good and right. Do we choose honesty and integrity in our budget, putting in place line-item budgeting to stop the blackmail, stop spending money we don't have, and cut spending and pay off our debt? Or do we keep spending money we don't have to create more debt, weakening the United States with each passing day?

Chapter 5: The Right to Life

For Thou didst form my inward parts; Thou didst weave me together in my mother's womb. I will give thanks to Thee, for I am fearfully and wonderfully made; wonderful are Thy works, and my soul knows it very well. Psalm 139:13,14 (NASV)

Intelligence Brief: A Baby's Right to Live and the Dangers of Abortions to Mothers

In the abortion debate, what voices are being heard? The voice of the baby cannot be heard at all unless an adult who has a voice speaks for the child. For this reason the case for the baby to have the right to life is given first in this chapter—in the first section—as it is usually the voice that is not heard by those who focus only on the rights of the mother.

The case for the mother's health and well-being in the abortion debate is made next—and the father's role is also addressed. The abortion procedure violates the natural development of a baby within a mother's womb and can be very dangerous medically to a woman. It can also be dangerous to her mental health. We often hear from women demanding the right to an abortion, but are we hearing the voices of women who have been injured, physically and psychologically, from abortions?

The voices of the women wanting abortions are voices most often heard in modern media. They may not want to be called mothers but the truth is, if dealing with the question of an abortion, a pregnant woman is the mother to the child that is growing within her. The voices of the mother may be heard in the press, but selectively, presenting only the side that supports the positions of the media source.

In the recent governor's race in Kentucky, a political TV advertisement presented the voice of a girl who was the victim of incest and how tragic it was for her to not be able to get an abortion in her state.[21] What about the voices of those who were raped and still had their child and that are now very thankful for a new human life that can be loved and nurtured? What about the voices of the children who have been born as a result of a rape and have gone on to live wonderful lives? I have heard these voices, and they are powerful because they champion the truth that another human life is in the abortion decision, and that life has value too.

If the only voices heard are those who demanded an abortion after a horrible crime, the voices of those who realized that there was a child in the balance and allowed the baby to be born may never be heard or considered. Certainly the voice of the baby in the womb is not going to be heard, because human babies take several years to develop before they can form words and sentences and thoughts. But babies can scream and cry and feel pain. They may not be able to organize and articulate their arguments, and pay for media campaigns, but babies are human beings, and have the protection of the right to life that is already clearly in the U.S. Constitution. Modern day opinions on these matters are turned in accordance with what voices are allowed to be heard by the gatekeepers of public information. What about the voice of the baby? What about the baby's position? The media frequently cries out about the rights of the mother, but what about the rights of the baby?

The Baby

From *Roe* to *Dobbs*, the question that has been asked over and over is this: "Does a woman have a Constitutional right to an abortion?" For anyone raising this right for a woman to have an abortion they by necessity open the door to the follow-on question: "Does a baby in a mother's womb have a right to life?" This is due to the scientific fact that an abortion unavoidably destroys another human life. What is the Constitutional right of the baby, and what is the true moral high ground that we seem so hesitant to champion?

Many who argue for abortion vary on when they consider a baby in the womb a baby with a right to life. The closer the baby gets to full term, the larger the number of people that agree that the baby has a life interest—a right to life. Some consider this question from the viewpoint that the mother has a fundamental liberty right to an abortion only to be denied if there is a compelling state interest (part of the Strict Scrutiny legal test). These consider the baby's life more of a compelling state interest worth protecting when the baby in the womb approaches a certain number of weeks old—possibly 6 weeks or beyond.[22] But we miss the more fundamental factual question, legal question, and the higher moral question, if we do not view this question from the baby's position.

Moving our perspective from the mother to the baby, we must see them both on equal footing as human beings, both with the right to life and liberty. The fundamental right to life for all people is guaranteed in the U.S. Constitution (Amendments 5 and 14). This is not about a compelling state interest to overcome the mother's liberty right. The mother has no liberty right to willfully take the life of another human being. People like to emphasize liberty and the freedom of the mother to control her future. But we do not have the freedom to do whatever we want—we don't have the freedom to harm other people. There are criminal laws against assault and murder. The baby in the womb is a human being and, like the mother, has a fundamental right to life guaranteed in our U.S. Constitution.

There has been such a one-sided focus on the mother's liberty interest in legal cases that the baby's interest has generally not even been addressed. For example, even in *Dobbs*, Clarence Thomas asked during oral argument whether there is a Constitutional right to an abortion for the mother (in *Dobbs* the U.S. Supreme Court held there is not a Constitutional right for an abortion), but none of the Supreme Court Justices of the United States, including Clarence Thomas, were willing to ask the follow-on question that screams for attention: "Does the baby in the womb have a Constitutional right to life?"[23] For those who demand we seriously consider their argument for a woman's Constitutional right to an abortion, they must understand that they open the door to the question of whether the baby in the womb has a Constitutional right to life, because in an abortion a human life is taken.

The question of the baby's Constitutional right to life turns on whether the child in the womb is a baby—a human person—and when? With sonograms and modern science most people agree that babies in the final weeks of pregnancy are clearly lives to be protected. Is the baby only a human life with human rights after a certain number of weeks—maybe after 26 weeks, or 25 weeks? Is the baby in the womb only a human person with a right to life at 15 weeks? What about at 12 weeks? What about 6 weeks, or 5 weeks? The scientific and moral answer is that the baby in the womb is a human being during all these weeks, and any person, judge, or legislator that wants to make the call on which week the child becomes a human life with the right to life, and which week they do not have the right to life, places themselves in the position of God Almighty. It is a known fact that when a man and a woman have sex together, they may physiologically produce a child, and that child is a human life from conception. It's not a collection of undefined cells, it is not another species of life, it is, in fact, a human life.

As with any other legal situation where one human life threatens another, we can apply the legal concept of self-defense to protect the mother's life in those rare situations where the baby's life threatens the life of the mother. When the mother's health is in danger doctors can work with their patients as they do with any medical situation where life is at risk. They do not require the court's intervention in such situations. They must use their best professional judgment, working with their patients, to make difficult decisions in those rare cases where the baby in the womb becomes dangerous to the mother's life. As with any case, and as with any profession, medical providers are open to legal review and possible legal challenge from those who may question whether they are giving appropriate care to preserve life. When anyone goes in for medical treatment in the United States, there are laws in place that provide protection from malpractice related injuries that could be caused by the intentional or negligent behavior of a medical provider that damages life and health rather than improves it.

The abortion debate is a moral debate. The moral position to stand for the baby's right to life takes us to a leadership opportunity very similar to what Abraham Lincoln faced with another major moral question in America—slavery. Those who were pro-slavery missed the moral question and were arguing for what they reasoned was good and best (in their eyes) for the slave owners. They viewed the slave as something less of a person than the slave owner. Those who took this position left a legacy of disgrace, and have blood on their hands for both the slaves who were mistreated and those who died at the hands of their owners—and to the 600,000 people who died in the U.S. Civil War over a moral issue that should have been decided through the lawmaking process of our constitutional republic by people who should have all agreed that every human being has the right to liberty (freedom).

Those who are pro-abortion are viewing the abortion question from the position of the mother—what is good and best (in their eyes) for the mother. They make the same mistake as those who fought for slavery in our Civil War because they refuse to consider the moral and constitutional rights of the one on the other side of the argument. This is "the fallacy of the Civil War South" we described back in Chapter 1. The obsession on one side of an argument prevents a truthful view of the other side. They are fighting to persuade the whole country to think only of the mother's liberty right and join them in their moral disgrace to abandon the cause of another human being involved in any abortion—the baby. Should we not, as a nation, unite on what is morally right and unite in the position that babies in the womb are human beings and they too have a Constitutional right to life?

We are now in a country where, on a critical moral question comparable to slavery, some states allow abortion (the killing of innocent children), and some states make it unlawful to kill children in the womb. Lincoln would not stand for a nation that was half free, and half in slavery. We ultimately united as a country to take the moral and legal high ground that slaves should be free, and all human beings have a constitutional right to life and liberty. The question should not have been so difficult, but it became horrifically difficult due to the narrow-minded thinking of those fighting for slavery who refused to acknowledge the rights of the slaves as human beings. As to one-sided blindness we are now in a very similar situation due to the narrow thinking of those so focused on the mother's right to liberty that they refuse to see that babies in the womb are human beings with the constitutional right, even now, to life and liberty and the pursuit of happiness.

Those fighting for abortion think it unthinkable that a woman who gets pregnant should be held legally accountable for having an abortion. The fact is that when a woman gets pregnant, she has another human life (sometimes multiple human lives) developing within her womb. Like it or not, she has become a mother. It may shock you to know this, but all over America, every day, in every jurisdiction that hears legal cases involving human beings, there are cases being heard of parents, mothers and fathers, who have killed their babies and children (that are already born). In some cases they have drowned them, purposely. In other cases they have shaken them so violently that they have killed them. In other cases they have struck them with such force or such repetition that they have killed them. The fact patterns are many, and each case is different. In some cases there is clear intent to take the child's life, in other cases there are various levels of negligence. In some cases there are facts that mitigate the culpability of the mother—she may have been under duress, or distracted, or having various psychological problems, or under the influence of drugs. Each case is unique. But in our U.S. courts every day there are parents being tried for the murder of their children. So as shocking as it may be to some to think about the possibility of holding mothers who are pregnant legally responsible for the killing of their child in an abortion, it should be made known that in our legal system today we are already holding parents responsible for killing their children. Babies, and children of all ages, are human beings with the right to life and if someone kills them, including their parents, whoever killed them should be subject to the same legal review that any person faces when they are involved in taking the life of another human being.

What about the terrible situation of rape or incest? Consider a situation, during the time of slavery, when a 13-year-old child is raped by her owner. The baby is born, and when it is one week old it is found. It is clearly the child of the slave-owner. Do we kill the baby because it was a child of rape? No, this would clearly be murder. What if we killed the child when it had been born the day before, or when it was 25 weeks in the womb, or, 20, or 10, or 5 weeks old in the womb? It would still be murder. Rape and incest are traumatic events, but do we want to add a second traumatic event to what the victim is already suffering—do we add to her burden to bear the killing of an innocent child? We do not go around killing children for the sins of their parents. The truth is the baby that is conceived from rape or incest is still a human being. To only consider the mother's situation, as bad as it may be, to the exclusion of the baby's situation—a live, innocent human life—is to deny the truth.

Two wrongs do not make a right. It is a horrific wrong for a girl to be raped. She will have to live with this trauma the rest of her life. Having an abortion puts her through a second traumatic event, the taking of an innocent life that will be a second unnecessary trauma for her to deal with for the rest of her life. I know of several cases where a woman was raped and put her child up for adoption. The child went on to live a wonderful life. If someone is to be killed or punished for the crime of rape or incest, punishment should be given to the rapist, not the baby that had no guilt in the crime.

In the presentation of the facts regarding abortion, the horrific torment that a baby goes through in an abortion must also be reported. Abortion procedures vary depending on how developed the baby is, but the purpose in every case includes killing a child. In some procedures, the baby is chopped up into pieces, as if put in a blender, so it can more easily be extracted. In other procedures, arms and legs are cut off. In other procedures the head is crushed. With other abortion options the child is poisoned. If somehow the baby makes it out alive, procedures may then include slitting the neck to make sure the baby is dead. And the baby is not given an anesthetic for any of this torture, for to take this extra step would make clear that the doctor is dealing with another human life. The baby has committed no crime, its only fault is that it is alive—yet abortion horrifically, painfully, takes the life of the baby.

Abortion requires the child to be killed—and killed in a terrible way.

This may not be nice to be factually honest about what happens in an abortion. But from the baby's position, abortion is not nice, it is painful, it is horrific, it is torture. It is way past time to stop being so nice to those so determined to fight for abortion. We must be factual about what happens in an abortion. We must call it what it is, the evil torture and killing of an innocent life. And the baby in the womb, like any baby in their first several years of life, is completely at the mercy of their caregiver, and completely unable to represent themselves in a court of law. Babies in the womb will never be heard unless adults do what is right and advocate for the clear Constitutional rights of these babies as human beings.

The Mother and Father

How much do people rallying for abortion truly care for what is best for the mother? We know they are not considering the baby, but do you hear them talk about the dangers of abortion to the mother? Several important health concerns and risks for the mother are involved in any abortion. The delicate, internal reproductive system of the mother is designed to develop a child. Once conceived, a baby starts a natural process of growth that occurs within a protected system designed to allow the baby to receive nutrition and biological support necessary for a human life. This support system of the mother involves a natural process that is designed to move forward the baby's development in a healthy, protected way. Generally, the healthiest thing for all involved is to let nature take its course.

In an abortion there is an interference with this natural process of a baby's development in the mother's womb. Of course the design in an abortion is to kill and remove the child from the womb, but this produces risks and potential harm to the mother's reproductive system and to her general health. Some of these risks include: pelvic infection, incomplete abortion complications (such as baby body parts left in the uterus, requiring future medical procedures), blood clots in the uterus, heavy bleeding (hemorrhaging), cut or torn cervix, perforation of the uterus wall, anesthesia-related complications, RH Immune Globulin complications, and future child bearing problems as a result of abortion complications or from having many abortions.[24] With some of these complications there is also the risk of death.[25]

If we are truly concerned with the physical health of the mother, it is important to be honest about the health risks for her that can result from an abortion. Before an abortion, the well-designed natural process of a baby developing in the womb is generally in place with a healthy mother and a healthy baby. Of course, abortion destroys the life of an otherwise healthy child, but abortion can also create numerous health concerns for the mother that would not have been an issue if nature's process had been left undisturbed.

There are also mental health concerns for mothers for their future as they must process multiple conflicting thoughts about their abortion(s). Though often told by modern "professionals" that an abortion will help them with their problems, many women have a lifetime of mental health struggles as a result of their decision(s) to abort their baby.[26]

If we truly are concerned about the mother in an abortion, we are not doing her any favors by shielding her from the immediate and future physical and mental/emotional dangers to her that result from an abortion.

Seldom considered in the abortion debate is the role of the father, or even the rights of the father. The father should be actively responsible for the care of the mother and the baby, from the baby's conception. He also is at the risk of mental trauma if his child is destroyed in an abortion.[27] More will be mentioned about the father's responsibilities in the next section. As we consider honest answers regarding human beings in the womb receiving the care they need we must consider the role of both the mother and the father.

Integrity First Answer: From Conception the Baby in the Womb Has a Constitutional Right to Life

If we have integrity, and truly care about the mother and the baby, we should be honest with any woman requesting an abortion. She should be clearly told that she carries another human life. She may have valid concerns about her current situation in her life, and that she may not have the time or resources to deal with a baby. But her own interests do not erase the fact that there is another living human being that is involved. She should be reassured that there are options like adoption, or possibly finding help from family members, to take custody of a baby if need be.

Instead of enabling a denial of the situation the mother is in, our society should love and embrace her to help her think beyond the difficult situation she is experiencing, to see the truth that another human life needs love and attention into the future, just as she does.

The father of the child should also be brought in to be of assistance. He should be required to pay bills and provide other support that may be required from the beginning of the pregnancy. The mother and father may not have wanted to have a child, but in the vast majority of pregnancies the sexual partners have willingly decided to engage in the very act that we all know can result in the formation of new human life. They have already made their free choice. Once we have a baby, we don't just kill it because it is an inconvenience to us. If the child is not wanted by the parents, there are pregnancy centers and churches and other non-profit organizations in most every community that can help those with unwanted pregnancies to make sure the baby has the care it needs. Even if help is not readily available this is not a reason to kill a child. Help should be sought, and new opportunities created where they may not have existed before for a baby that needs care.

The mother that is pregnant, and the father that was a partner in the decision that resulted in the creation of new human life, should be informed (if they didn't already know) that, in America, we honor the moral truth that all human beings have a God-given right to life. This is in our U.S. Constitution now—so taking the life of the child should not be an option, unless that child is a threat to the mother's health.

As to those in America fighting for abortion, the Integrity First Answer is to first honestly communicate to them that fighting for the killing of innocent children places them on the wrong moral side of the question. There may be many fighting for abortion, as there were many fighting for slavery in the U.S. Civil War, but as those who fought for slavery were on the wrong side of the moral question by thinking only of the rights of the slave owners, those who fight for abortion are on the wrong side of the moral question by fighting only for the rights of the mother. Their position is just as wrong morally as those who fought for slavery. History already shows they hold a disgraceful position that ignores the now existing constitutional right of an innocent child to have life.

As to incest, and rape, we have one horrific traumatic event for the victim. We do her no favor by adding a second traumatic event in the killing of an innocent child. If we start killing children for the sins of their fathers, there is no end to the murders of innocent children that would result. If we have integrity, we understand that with rape or incest, as bad as those crimes are, the inescapable truth is we still have a new human life that morally should not be murdered. With anyone demanding an abortion, we must be honest and communicate that the mother is not the only human being with rights that must be considered.

The Integrity First Answer is that the baby, as a human being, has the same right to life that we all enjoy, guaranteed in the 5th and 14th Amendments of the current U.S. Constitution. The U.S. Supreme Court should take on the next abortion case that is appealed, and not just hold that the mother does not have a constitutional right to an abortion as it did in *Dobbs*, but hold that babies in the womb, from conception, are human beings with the constitutional right to life. The baby in the womb is a human being who has the same right to life as any other baby or child. Their life or death is in the hands of their caregivers. This dependency for life and proper care begins at conception.

Consistent with long standing current law that applies whenever the life of one human being is being threatened by another human being, when the mother's physical health would be seriously at risk from the baby, decisions can be made to protect the life of the mother.

If the U.S. Supreme Court fails to take on a case and honor the facts and the law about the baby in the womb being a human being with a right to life, the Integrity First Answer for the U.S. Congress would be to pass legislation that babies from conception have the right to life, per the U.S. Constitution, with an exception when the mother's physical health would be seriously at risk. But do we have such leaders of integrity in the U.S. Congress?

The Integrity First Answer for the President would be to sign a pro-life bill into law and enforce it by holding the medical community to the same standard of saving lives in the womb as is currently law for any other human being in America—to preserve life, not destroy it. The President also has the power to sign a proclamation, as Lincoln did with his Emancipation Proclamation, that all human life in the womb is protected life under the U.S. Constitution. But this will take a President with the courage of Lincoln.

If needed, the integrity first answer may require the passing of a U.S. Constitutional Amendment to clarify that abortion takes the life of an innocent child, and is unconstitutional under the U.S. Constitution, as all people have the right to life and liberty (unless they threaten the life of another). The 13th Amendment was passed to make clear that slaves were to be released as all people have the right to life and liberty. An Amendment may be required to clarify that babies in the womb, like any other people, have the right to life. As a matter of law this would not be required if we had a Supreme Court, President, and Congress, that honored the facts—babies in the womb are human beings and according to the U.S. Constitution, right now, human beings have a constitutional right to life.

As noted above, with modern medicine's ability to protect both the mother and the child, it is not common that a child in the womb will pose a serious risk to the mother, but when this does occur our medical providers must use the same standards of care they use when treating anyone in need. It should again be noted in this Integrity First Answer section, while most medical providers provide quality medical care, their actions are always subject to review, and we have a legal system in place in America to address conflicts between opposing positions. As with any legal cases where children without representation are involved, in contested cases involving the death or injury to a child, an attorney ad litem should be appointed to represent the interests of the child.

This is not a time for compromise on the abortion question. America should not be a nation where one state stands for the life of the child while another state stands for the death of the child, any more than we should have one state that stands for freedom while another state stands for slavery.

This is the leadership of Lincoln—in a time of great division, taking the side of truth and integrity, leading us to unity in what is morally good and right. Do we honor the truth that the baby in the womb, from conception, is a human being with the same right to life and liberty as anyone else? Or do we disregard the baby's right to life and liberty and think only of the mother's liberty interest? Do we unify in what is true and right, that a baby in the womb is, in fact, a human life? Or do we stay divided in support of lies and the murder of innocent children?

Chapter 6: The Afghanistan Withdrawal

"Intelligence, patriotism, Christianity, and a firm reliance on Him, who has never yet forsaken this favored land, are still competent to adjust, in the best way, all our present difficulty."[28] Abraham Lincoln

Intelligence Brief: The Hasty Withdrawal from Afghanistan Aided and Armed Our Enemies

In early July of 2021, the U.S. President announced that the withdrawal of United States military forces in Afghanistan would conclude by August 31, 2021.[29] As to the timing of this process, he did not take the advice of many senior military leaders (though he did take the advice of some who later softened from their original objections), but instead, he demanded a hasty evacuation of U.S. personnel. This reckless evacuation of our military forces in Afghanistan allowed the terrorist-supporting Taliban to quickly re-take the ground paid for by U.S. lives and bloodshed. The abrupt evacuation left massive amounts of U.S. military equipment in the hands of our enemies, and resulted in the needless death of 13 more Americans to add to the over 2300 American lives lost over the last 20 years in a freedom-fighting cause that was all disgracefully surrendered by President Biden and our senior military leadership.[30]

Our senior military leaders knew, or should have known, that a hasty withdrawal would be a disaster, and would allow our enemies to regain all the territory that had been won at great cost to American lives. All that we had gained was given back to our enemies.

We must have the courage to be honest about the way the withdrawal from Afghanistan was conducted. Though our military members who executed their withdrawal orders did so with valor, saving many Americans and Afghans by flying them out of the country, the orders from President Biden accomplished what many of our military leaders knew would happen—our enemies would be given back all that we had won (won at great cost to American and Afghan lives), and our enemies would be further advantaged by our leaving behind billions of dollars' worth of military equipment. We also know more American and Afghan lives were lost in the rapid reckless withdrawal of our forces. We must be honest about this. This was aiding the enemy, this was treason.

We cannot hide behind the veil of this being the policy of our President. It may have been the policy of our President and others that supported him, but, pulling back the veil, the policy clearly resulted in giving U.S enemies back all that we had gained, arming them with our own military equipment, and allowing them to further promote terrorism against the United States. If you want to call it the President's policy, it was a policy of treason, and those at the top who were responsible, civilian and military, should face legal prosecution for treason.

Treason is clearly defined in the U.S. Constitution, Article 3, Section 3 to include "adhering to their Enemies" and giving them "Aid and Comfort." There is no question in fact that the hasty withdrawal from Afghanistan greatly advantaged our enemies.

The right thing to do when Americans have fought and died in support of freeing a nation from tyrants, as we did with Germany and Japan in World War II and with Korea in the Korean War, is to have numerous other nations joining us in our cause against a tyrannical enemy, assuring our strength and success. With combined forces working together victory can be achieved to avoid a long and drawn out war. After defeating the enemy U.S. forces can maintain a presence in the country we have freed to prevent the loss of what has been gained, and help them to build and maintain a free nation that is no longer an enemy but an ally to the United States. We still have U.S. forces on the ground in Germany, Japan, and Korea, and we maintain supportive relationships with these nations. In contrast to this plan for victory over tyrannical governments we followed the same disgraceful policy in Afghanistan as we did in Vietnam.

In our training at the Air Force Academy we were taught that, among the many lessons learned from Vietnam, we had U.S. military senior leaders following military policy given to them from civilian leaders that denied military success. This unlawfully and immorally resulted in a long and drawn-out conflict which betrayed those fighting for freedom, and ultimately resulted in defeat and the reckless loss of American and International lives. Senior military leaders should have been pushing back on such unlawful policies, and should have demanded proven strategies for victory be followed, or they should have resigned in protest. Instead, military leaders were more concerned with their own selfish promotions in rank rather than defeating our enemies. When sending Americans to their death in war there must be a plan for victory, not defeat. Giving back to our enemies all we had fought for in Vietnam was certainly aiding the enemy, it was treason, and senior civilian and military leaders should have been held accountable through impeachment or other legal process.

Our senior leaders made the same mistakes in Afghanistan that were made in Vietnam. We should have taken lessons from our success in Korea. If we were going to be in Afghanistan plans should have been made for victory, not defeat, including the involvement of other nations to help us in our cause. In Korea: "Out of 59 nations then in the UN, 48 offered aid or troops to help defend South Korea. Seven non-UN members also sent aid. Adding Japan and Germany—both still under Allied occupation but also pitching in—and South Korea itself, the US-led coalition amounted to 58 nations. Over 20 had 'boots on the ground.' "[31] Our opportunities for success increase when we have numerous other countries with us. This did not happen in Vietnam, and it did not happen in Afghanistan. This is because of poor leadership at the top and reckless disregard for what it takes to win international conflicts.

In Afghanistan, Americans fought against terrorists, with thousands upon thousands of Afghans who wanted to be free from the tyrannical rule of the Taliban. We should have had other nations that share our love for freedom fighting with us—as we did in World War II and in Korea. We should have defeated our enemy in the first year or two of our deployments there and helped Afghanistan to be a free nation where we maintain a military presence, just as we have done with Germany, Japan, and Korea. In contrast to this, President Biden clearly stated that his policy in Afghanistan was not to help build Afghanistan into a nation of freedom and success like other nations we have helped free from a tyrant's rule.[32] Instead, he gave back to our enemies all we had fought and died for in Afghanistan, and left our enemies billions of dollars' worth of U.S. military equipment. Now power over the entire nation is back with the Taliban who can once again support terrorism against the United States. Not only our President but also the senior leaders who carried out his orders, granted assistance and success to our enemies, which is treasonous.

Reports and testimony from some senior leaders suggest that they thought Afghanistan military forces could defend themselves without the help of the United States, as was also the rationale given by President Biden.[33] This denies the lessons learned from Germany, Japan, and Korea, that after winning decisive victories against an enemy, U.S. forces must be maintained in countries to ensure what has been won is not lost. If the poor judgment of our senior military leaders was not willful treason, it was in the alternative criminal recklessness.

You may be asking, why take such a strong stance against our military leaders? Go to the dedication page. We must stop sending Americans to give their lives fighting for the cause of freedom against dangerous tyrants, and then give up everything gained by American bloodshed and sacrifice to the benefit of our enemies. This is not what we did fighting foreign wars in World War I and World War II. This is the opposite of honor and integrity. If we send Americans to their death to fight for freedom we should take the course of victory, not defeat. In doing this we honor the service of the Americans who gave their all. To do otherwise has aided our enemies in their tyranny, and it is treason. We made this mistake in Vietnam, and we made the same mistake in Afghanistan. We have probable cause to hold our senior leadership accountable and they should be tried for treason.

Integrity First Answer: Congress Should Demand Prosecution of Treason and High Crimes

When senior military leaders were given treasonous orders they should have had the integrity to demand alternative plans, and made it clear to the President that they could not execute unlawful, criminal orders. This act of honor alone could have shown the President the error of his ways, but instead they carried out the treason. In the alternative, if our senior officers had integrity they should have resigned their positions before carrying out criminal orders. In facing court martial or other legal process they could have made clear their defense for all to see: that they would not join the President in his treason.

Another opportunity for senior leaders after their resignation in protest would have been for them to take their case immediately to the Congress. They also could have publicized the treason of the President's orders, taking their case to the American people. This is what can happen in a country where there is freedom of speech and freedom of the press. All voices should be heard—those who agree with the government leadership, but also those who oppose it.

The famous case of the court martial of General Billy Mitchel stands as a great example of a senior leader who stood tall against the reckless policies of those over him. After World War I, General Billy Mitchel demonstrated with great clarity the power of the airplane to destroy land and naval forces, and that the U.S. military should have invested heavily in airpower. Instead, Army and Navy senior leaders ignored his position. General Mitchel took a stand against their criminal recklessness which at that time had resulted in the death in crashes of several airmen, and he predicted (accurately, as time would tell) that Japan was preparing for a surprise attack on Hawaii, using air power. The personal cost to Billy Mitchel was high as he was court-martialed, demoted, and forced out of the military. But history has shown he was absolutely right in his position.[34] Oh that we would have had some Billy Mitchel's that had stood up against the criminal orders they were given by President Biden to leave Afghanistan with such reckless haste.

When our senior military commanders were given unlawful orders and joined the President in his treason, the only other body of government that could have resolved the problem was the U.S. Congress. The Congress has held hours of testimony about the Afghanistan withdrawal disaster, but they must do more than just talk about the mistakes that were made.[35] Where clear evidence exists of serious crimes committed against our nation by U.S. senior military leaders, Congress should conduct full legal proceedings and hold them accountable Legal process should be undertaken to make public all criminal behavior and demand prosecution for treason, as determined by the facts, of all those responsible, using impeachment and other appropriate legal proceedings.

In the United States the remedy for treason committed by top executive branch leaders is clearly described in our U.S. Constitution. It's found in Article 2, Section 4: "The President, Vice President and all civil Officers of the United States, shall be removed from Office on Impeachment for, and Conviction of, Treason, Bribery, or other high Crimes and Misdemeanors." Treason is clearly on the list for impeachable crimes.

This hasty retreat not only restored our terrorist enemies to power in Afghanistan and armed them with U.S.

military equipment, but it also sent a message to our other enemies, including Russia, China, Iran, and North Korea, that the United States was no longer going to stand against terrorists and tyrants. We now have wars going on with Russia attacking Ukraine and HAMAS and other terrorist organizations attacking Israel. We can only wonder who China and Iran may attack next. Instead of experiencing peace through strength, we are experiencing war through weakness. When the U.S. is strong, the world is much more secure; when the U.S. is weak the world is much more dangerous.

The treason committed by our President will be addressed more in Chapter 9, but if the U.S. House of Representatives was acting with integrity it should have impeached the President and the U.S. Secretary of Defense for carrying out the hasty Afghanistan withdrawal. The U.S. Senate should then have conducted full trials to present evidence of this treason for all to see, giving each member of the Senate the opportunity to apply the facts to the law.

To legally hold those guilty of crimes against our nation accountable takes a great deal of courage and work from Congress and this may not be politically popular, but it is the Integrity First Answer to a military with criminal or reckless leadership. This same high level of legal review should have happened in Vietnam, and there should be legal accountability for the treason and/or recklessness conducted by civilian and military leaders in the quick withdrawal from Afghanistan.

Both our senior civilian leadership committed treason, and our senior military leaders also committed treason in carrying out such a criminal, unlawful, and disastrous retreat out of Afghanistan. This is not just a matter of a President making a bad policy decision. This is not just about Democrats or Republicans getting their political way. When the President is committing treason, and the military senior leadership is joining the treason, the integrity first answer would be for our U.S. Congress to do their job, exercise active oversight over the actions of our top U.S. military leaders, and do more than just talk about the crimes that occurred via hours of oversight hearings. For the disgraceful withdrawal from Afghanistan, top U.S. military leaders should have been prosecuted for executing orders that were criminal and treasonous, even if it took setting up a special independent tribunal as we have for the prosecution of other war crimes. If the appropriate legal process shows treason was committed we must hold our senior leadership accountable for such costly criminal behavior so future military commanders know they will be held accountable for similar poor judgment.

This is strong moral courage—in a time of great division, taking the side of truth and integrity, leading us to unity in what is morally good and right. Do we honor the truth about Afghanistan, recognizing that what our President and senior civilian and military leaders did in the rapid abandonment of the U.S. mission to defeat terrorism substantially aided our enemy and was treason? Or do we choose to ignore their crimes that dishonored all who died in this cause and that put back into power the terror-sponsoring Taliban? If there was any doubt that the Taliban was our enemy, they proved it by the number of Americans they killed and injured through the years we were there in Afghanistan. Yet we gave up all that was gained through American sacrifice and re-armed our enemy with American weapons and machines of war. Do we unify in what is true and right, to hold accountable those senior civilian and military leaders that committed treason? Or do we stay divided to allow the senior leaders in charge of this withdrawal to deny the truth that the withdrawal, in the manner it was ordered, planned, and conducted, clearly aided our enemies?

Chapter 7: The Chinese Spy Balloon

"If a ruler listens to lies, all his officials become wicked."
Proverbs 29:12

Intelligence Brief: A Chinese Spy Balloon Was Allowed to Fly Over U.S. Military Bases

From January 28 to February 4, 2023, a Chinese Balloon entered U.S. airspace without permission—this was a violation of U.S. Federal Regulations.[36] It clearly traveled over numerous U.S. military installations that are of great importance to our military strategic nuclear defense.[37] This was no accident. This was no random journey of a weather balloon. The U.S. military knew about it or clearly should have known about it, when it was over the Pacific Ocean and heading into North American Airspace.

The work I did in the United States Air Force included pulling alert duty in Iceland where we actively scrambled U.S. aircraft to intercept Soviet aircraft heading into North American Airspace. During that time we actively intercepted unidentified aircraft coming into North America, with special attention to aircraft coming from communist countries. We sent fighter aircraft to physically intercept, identify, and turn away Soviet aircraft before they entered North American airspace.[38] Our U.S. aircraft were fully armed, and we all knew that intentional violation of United States airspace by military or potentially dangerous aerospace vehicles would be considered an act of aggression and possibly an act of war. Aircraft determined to be dangerous would be destroyed if they did not turn back before they flew over the North American landmass where they could have released weapons or done other damage to the United States.

The large Chinese spy balloon that flew across the United States was clearly from China.[39] Our basic U.S. air defense policy calls for such air traffic that could be a threat to the United States to be intercepted and identified.[40] The aerospace vehicle was known to be from China, but its cargo was unknown at first and therefore could have been a weapons system or spy system. Because of these dangers it should have been intercepted and destroyed before it violated U.S. Airspace—before it did any further damage to our country.[41]

The evidence shows we did not know what the balloon was carrying, but we did know it was large enough to have been carrying a weapon.[42] If this was a weapon, it could have been disastrous, and so it should have been treated as dangerous and destroyed before it came into U.S. airspace. After being allowed to fly completely over the United States northern sections it was finally shot down. We know now that it was carrying high-tech surveillance equipment. It was a spy balloon collecting intelligence information by traveling over sensitive U.S. military bases, confirming that we were only helping the enemy by allowing them to have a trial run of flying directly over critical strategic U.S. bases that house nuclear weapons.[43]

Integrity First Answer: Congress Should Hold Civilian and Military Leaders Accountable

The Balloon never should have entered U.S. airspace. To allow it to collect intelligence by flying over sensitive military bases, including several of our strategic nuclear missile facilities, was aiding the enemy, and we must call it what it is, treason. At the least, it is criminal recklessness or dereliction of duty.

The U.S. Congress should have exercised oversight over senior military leaders who lacked the integrity to do their jobs, and this oversight should have resulted in more than talk in oversight hearings. If Congress doesn't hold our senior civilian and military commanders accountable for unlawful conduct, no one else will. Congress should have impeached senior civilian leaders and demanded the prosecution of senior military officers for criminal conduct, in military or criminal court, for allowing a Chinese spy balloon to fly a course that took it over our military bases assisting our enemies in achieving their military objectives.

In a time of great division as to what it means to defend our borders, we need leaders with moral courage, taking the side of truth and integrity, leading us to unity in what is morally good and right. Do we protect our nation from dangerous aircraft that fly into our country to threaten and spy on our nation? Do we hold those who refused to protect us accountable? Or do we allow criminal recklessness, dereliction of duty and treason to continue in the support of our enemies and their agendas?

Chapter 8: The HAMAS Terrorist Attack on Israel

"Bloodthirsty men hate a man of integrity and seek to kill the upright." Proverbs 29:10

Intelligence Brief: The HAMAS Attack on Israel Puts HAMAS in the Same Place as the Nazis

On October 7, 2023, HAMAS conducted a terrorist attack on Israel. Women were raped and killed, babies were killed and beheaded, children were raped and killed, whole families were killed, men were killed and beheaded; and babies, children, women, and men were taken hostage.[44] The victims include more than 1400 Israeli civilians and soldiers murdered, 32 Americans murdered, and at least 11 Americans feared to be with over 200 hostages held by HAMAS (as of the time of this writing).[45] These innocent people were targets for one reason, because they were Jewish.

We have seen this horrific disregard for human life before. Calling someone a Nazi has been way overused and misused in our society, but in the actual history of this group we clearly now know that a group of Germans, the Nazis, carried out horrific violence on the Jewish people. The Nazis decided they needed to exterminate all Jewish people, and they killed millions of Jews in their reign of terror. Though the majority of the German people may not have officially become Nazis, the country of Germany and her leadership went along with them.[46] History has clearly surfaced the facts of the horror and terror of the Nazis killing millions of innocent people, including women, children and the elderly. It is now a great embarrassment, recorded in the history of the German people, that they supported the Nazis.

The world was left with a clear moral mandate to come after the Nazis in World War II, which meant coming after all who supported them in the nation of Germany. The same principle applies in war that applies in criminal justice. If you have evil people in your town, city, or state who are killing innocent people, the government has the duty to seek out and put an end to the deadly criminal conduct. As much as we would like everyone to get along and have peaceful resolutions to evil behavior, when someone shows their determination to kill innocent people it is not the time to be nice and bring out the social architects—unless you want more people to be killed. It's time to send out law enforcement who carry weapons to be used against those determined to be violent killers.

We find a similar circumstance with HAMAS today. They have shown their determination, again, to kill Jews and Americans. They have committed mass murder tactics that take us right back to the behavior of the Nazis. Those who commit and support this level of terror cannot be corrected by negotiation, but must be stopped by military force and criminal prosecution.

A large number of people in the world today are supporting the Palestinians who are supporting HAMAS; just as there were a large number of people supporting the Germans who were supporting the Nazis when they began their reign of terror. Just as it was a time for taking sides when the Nazis began their reign of terror, this is a time for taking sides, and many people are showing their misinformed and reckless foolishness in taking the side of Palestinians who are in support of HAMAS. As with the war against Germany, we have an active war now against HAMAS which was elected to leadership by the majority of the Palestinian people. In conducting a war against an evil nation, all the atrocities of war will be found, including the killing of innocent people on both sides. But we did not have any doubt who started the entire evil mess in World War II, it was Nazi Germany. And the Nazis had to be defeated. The Nazis could have ended the war at any time if they had surrendered—it was in their hands to stop the fighting—but until they surrendered they were facing all the destruction of war they brought upon themselves.

We know clearly who started the war now going on against Israel, it was HAMAS Palestinians, backed by Iran. As long as HAMAS, and other neighboring terrorists supporting them, are in power in Palestine, or anywhere else, they must be defeated. They can end the war at any time if they would surrender—it is in their hands. Those thousands of people who are taking the side of the Palestinians in support of HAMAS in this war are on the wrong side of history, as they are siding with an evil enemy who has made their terrorism very clear for all to see. For those crying out for peace and ending the war in Israel, HAMAS and the Palestinians that support them can end the war at any time by laying down their arms. They must end the terror, surrender, and face the criminal justice proceedings that await those who have committed such evil. But, like the Nazis, HAMAS has shown its true colors, and all who are standing to support them are showing their true colors, in support of the evil and terror of HAMAS—as long as they keep fighting and killing people they must be militarily defeated.

The majority of the world was slow to understand the dangers of the Nazis. Most nations appeased them, gave them what they wanted, and let them carry out their terror taking one peaceful nation after another, starting with Poland. After years of allowing the Nazis to have their evil way, the world finally united against them and destroyed them. When America finally got involved, we all knew it was a time of war. It's a shame the U.S. didn't see the seriousness of the Nazi threat when the Germans first took Poland. Imagine how different things could have been if the U.S. and the world joined forces to defeat Germany when the Nazis first attacked Poland in 1939.

During our war against the Nazis the U.S. would not have considered sending any kind of aid, humanitarian or otherwise, to the German people in Nazi Germany. The Nazis were in charge. Any assistance sent would have gone in the hands of the Nazis to help their effort. The Nazis could have surrendered at any time—their future was in their hands—but as long as they were fighting against us, our mission was to defeat them, not assist them in their terror.

We must be honest with the facts and know the attack on Israel by HAMAS is a direct result of support HAMAS has received from Iran.[47] What is both treasonous and horrific is that Iran's power, and therefore the power of HAMAS, is a direct result of billions of dollars of U.S. payments to Iran from U.S. leaders like Presidents Obama and Biden.[48] Since President Biden first took office Iran has also been allowed to make billions of dollars from its illicit oil sales.[49] The U.S. is clearly enabling Iran's leaders to continue to finance international terrorism. Can you imagine if the U.S. and other nations fighting against the Nazis had been simultaneously trading with them and supporting them? If we have the integrity to be honest, we must be truthful and note that we have had U.S. political leaders who were actively engaging in the treason of aiding and funding Iran and Palestine during a time of war.[50] These are disastrous failures of U.S. executive and legislative branch leadership. We would never have considered aiding Germany during the time of World War II. Our mission was to first defeat their evil leaders and war machine, then we could help rebuild their country, which we did. Once terrorist forces are defeated America can help countries get back on their feet, but we should not be supporting policies that are funding our enemies while these terrorist forces have yet to be defeated.

It is important to honestly note the bigger picture of executive branch failed leadership. The U.S. withdrawal from Afghanistan restored power to terrorists and gave Russia greater confidence to attack Ukraine. This U.S. weakness has also encouraged China to accelerate her rapid preparation for war. HAMAS, baked by Iran, has attacked Israel, and now Israel is at war with HAMAS, other Islamic terrorists, and Iran itself. We have been experiencing the opposite of peace through U.S. strength. We have been experiencing horrific wars due to U.S. weakness.

Integrity First Answer: The U.S. Should Demand the Hostages Be Released and Destroy Hamas and other Terrorist Organizations

Unfortunately, there have been times in history when war has been required so there can be future peace and freedom. War was required in America to defeat a brutal British monarch so that a new nation could have freedom and peace. War was required to defeat slavery in the U.S. Civil war, so there could be freedom and peace. War was required to defeat enemies of peace and freedom in both World War I and World War II. War was fought to defeat deadly enemies in Korea, Vietnam, Iraq, and Afghanistan. In the Korean War the U.S. fought, with the help of 50 other nations, to defeat a communist aggressor and secure freedom and peace for South Korea. In contrast, the United States surrendered to her dangerous enemies in Vietnam and Afghanistan due to treasonous poor leadership from the U.S. executive Branch (see Chapter 4), who failed to secure the help of 50 plus other nations to defeat a common enemy.

HAMAS has taken up the same tactics as the Nazis, and must be met with war-winning multinational forces determined to defeat HAMAS and other terrorist organizations that support HAMAS. Because Americans were killed and taken hostage, and because what HAMAS did was a criminal violation of international law, a strong U.S. response should already have included a quick strike from the U.S. to substantially destroy HAMAS military leaders. There should have also been an immediate demand for a return of those who were captured or greater damage would be inflicted on Iran. There should also be active prosecution of all those committing war crimes. But we did not have a strong and decisive response. Instead, with President Biden we had a weak and treasonous President who was responsible for funding and arming the terrorists through U.S. direct support to Iran and through pro-Iran economic policies, making Iran wealthy so they could continue to supply and fund HAMAS and other terrorist groups.

History has shown the evil of those who supported the Nazis and Germany in their terror. Those supporting HAMAS, including Iran and the Palestinians who celebrate terrorism, are making the same disgraceful and deadly mistake. When terrorists make themselves known we cannot support them; we must destroy them. Unpunished crime results in more crime. Many made the mistake of seeking the way of tolerance and compromise with the Nazis during their reign of terror, which only led to more Nazi-directed terror. We must have the wisdom and courage to call what HAMAS has done evil and criminal, and the world should unite in the war that is ongoing against such terrorists, as we united to defeat Nazi Germany. Terrorism is not nice, and our response to it must not be nice but must be swift and strong. This would take strong U.S. leadership, leaders who, instead of supporting our enemies, stand for what is right and inspire other nations to join us against an evil enemy.

Innocent families and children must be given warnings to leave areas that will be attacked. But if the terrorists are using these innocent people as human shields, the terrorists' horrific practices make it even more clear that they must be defeated. Fighting dangerous criminals cannot be done by appeasement. This is not a time to support Palestinians who celebrate HAMAS and who celebrate terrorism. They are choosing who they support; we must choose who we support. This is a time for Americans to unite in our fight against terrorism and unite against all who condone it.

The U.S. President who continues to allow Iran to earn billions in its unhindered sale of oil is at fault, and other U.S.

executive branch leaders are also at fault for aiding and abetting our enemies in Palestine and Iran, and for continuing to advance policies that weaken our nation; the Congress is at fault for not holding executive branch leaders responsible for their crimes, for sending money to Iran and Palestine that ends up funding HAMAS and other terrorist organizations, and for putting our nation in a position of even greater weakness by spending trillions of dollars we don't have and putting our nation at greater peril each day with ever increasing debt, now over $34 trillion; and U.S. voters are at fault for electing weak leaders that have lost sight of their primary responsibilities to support and defend the U.S. Constitution and the freedom from tyranny that is at the heart of it.

It all comes down to leadership. Elections have consequences. May God help us open our eyes. With his help may we stop electing leaders of foolishness, lies, weakness, and evil. May we instead elect leaders of integrity who champion wisdom, truth, goodness, and peace through strength.

This is the leadership of Lincoln—in a time of great division, taking the side of truth and integrity, leading us to unity in what is morally good and right. Do we stand with honor to defend those who have been raped, killed, tortured, beheaded, and taken hostage by terrorists committed to killing Jews and Americans? Or do we stand with those who support this horrific terrorism by those sworn to kill Jews and Americans? We have been through this before with Nazi Germany. Do we unify in what is true and right, or do we stay divided in support of lies and evil?

Chapter 9: The United States Department of Justice

Evil men do not understand justice, but those who seek the Lord understand it fully.
Proverbs 28:5

Intelligence Brief: The United States Department of Justice Has Become a Tool In the Hands of Political Liberals to Go After Political Conservatives

The history of our federal law enforcement agencies, including the FBI and other Department of Justice agencies and offices, includes many years of honorable service by the brave Americans that work to fight against dangerous criminals. Unfortunately, the history of these agencies also includes years of political bias by those in leadership, where DOJ agencies have clearly targeted the political enemies of executive branch leadership. As with any branch of the military, as with any police force, as with any federal executive branch agency, the quality and integrity of the organization is dependent upon the leadership. In the following paragraphs evidence of political bias in the Department of Justice is listed. All are clear evidence of major failures of the executive branch and DOJ leadership.

In the Hillary Clinton email investigation, during the time she was the United States Secretary of State, the FBI clearly discovered reckless mishandling of classified Information and obstruction of justice in the destruction of mobile devices and the use of BleachBit software to delete data from hard drives on laptops.[51] I know from my time in the Air Force that such treatment of classified information would be considered a criminal act and the end of any service member's career. However, in that case, acting FBI Director James Comey, with his cloak of prosecutorial discretion, "did not recommend any criminal charges to be filed against the Democratic presidential candidate."[52]

The FBI actively conspired with Hillary Clinton in the use of manufactured and paid for false evidence used before the U.S. Foreign Intelligence Surveillance (FISA) Court, alleging collusion between Russia and Trump in the 2016 election. Prior to the initial FBI FISA application containing false allegations, "the FBI in fact knew Steele (an FBI agent) had told Handling Agent-I that Fusion GPS had been hired by a law firm and that his ultimate client was 'senior Democrats supporting Clinton...' Moreover, it knew that Handling Agent-I's notes of this meeting reflect that, according to Steele, 'HC' (Hillary Clinton) was aware of his (Steele's) reporting."[53] The FBI knowingly used unverified evidence that clearly turned out to be a fabrication concocted from the Hillary Clinton campaign to suggest improper Russian collusion with Donald Trump. All of this was going on during the active 2016 presidential campaign where the motives and activities of the FBI were unquestionably working together to falsely discredit Donald Trump, the Democrat Party's opponent, and the opponent of Hillary Clinton.

FBI documents have been released clearly showing that the FBI plotted to ensnare retired General Michael Flynn with classic entrapment, creating a crime of misrepresentation and Russian collusion which was all the design of the FBI, not General Flynn.[54] The FBI was determined to further the agenda of the Democrat Party in the destruction of a political opponent, fabricating a crime in support of a political party rather than fighting actual crime.

As for the 2020 presidential election, one major group in the U.S is convinced that any illegal election activity that may have occurred in the U.S. November 2020 election was harmless error, and the election results can be trusted. Another major group is convinced that evidence clearly shows illegal election activity changed the 2020 election results. Article I, Section 4, gives state legislative bodies the primary authority to determine election laws used for local, state, and federal elections. But who is responsible for enforcing these laws?

While city, county, and state governments may enforce laws with their own state judicial systems, federal law clearly gives an enforcement role to the U.S. Department of Justice, especially in national elections. According to D.O.J.'s Election Crimes Branch: "The federal government asserts jurisdiction over an election offense to ensure that basic rights of United States citizenship, and a fundamental process of representative democracy, remain un-corrupted."[55] Our federal law-enforcement agencies are in the best position to enforce and prosecute illegal election activity where state corruption exists. Reasons for this include the "resources ….. required for successful prosecution," and the need for "detachment from local political forces."[56]

As much as we may not want the federal government involved in our local and state affairs, if local and state officials from one party are breaking election laws, can we trust them to use local and state law enforcement agents to prosecute the unlawful election conduct that put them in power? How else can this unlawful conduct be prosecuted if the federal D.O.J. does not step in? The U.S. Department of Justice's role is that of an umpire, or referee, to ensure election laws are enforced. Anyone competing in sports knows the critical importance of having unbiased officials cry "foul" when rules are broken. When it comes to U.S. elections, is the D.O.J. honoring this role?

Another way to look at the DOJ role is to remember the basic role of the DOJ and FBI is to enforce laws. To illustrate this principle of enforcement, consider what happens if it becomes known that the speed limit is not being enforced on a stretch of highway: drivers will actively disregard the speed limit. On the other hand, as often happens with a road that goes through a school zone, where there is active enforcement of the speed limit there will be very few speeders. This is the basic principle of enforcement—laws that are enforced will substantially be honored, and laws that are not enforced will be substantially ignored and broken.

In cities and states where there has not been active enforcement of election law violations at the city and state level, the FBI is responsible for prosecuting election law violations, per the DOJ policy referenced above.[57] Election laws have not been actively enforced at the state level in the battle-ground states of Arizona, Michigan, Pennsylvania, Wisconsin, Illinois, and Georgia. Civil suits have been attempted in some cases, but there is a general lack of enforcement of criminal election law corruption—the attorneys responsible for prosecuting criminal laws are government attorneys, not private attorneys. A September 2023 report notes these few voter fraud convictions from the 2020 election, at the state level: Arizona, 9; Michigan, 5; Pennsylvania, 6; Wisconsin, 9; Illinois, 1; and Georgia, 0.[58] For there to be active election law enforcement in the cities of these states we should expect to find more than just a few election law convictions during an election cycle. So since there is such little enforcement at the state level, is there evidence of active federal FBI enforcement of election law violations in these battleground states?

Consider the months following the November 2020 election. From November 3, 2020, through July 2021, of over 5000 F.B.I. press releases reporting FBI activity, five can be found dealing with election law enforcement, with no reporting of any convictions for election law violations stemming from the November 2020 elections.[59]

We know the DOJ is capable of enforcement, because we can see the DOJ's active enforcement actions after the January 6, 2021, rioting in Washington, D.C. In the months following this event, from January 6 through July, 2021, over 95 press releases can be found showing the F.B.I.'s high priority of enforcing laws broken on January 6. DOJ prosecution of cases on the January 6, 2021 event shows 623 people who have received sentences, over 378 people who have been sentenced to periods of incarceration, and 657 individuals who have pleaded guilty to federal charges, "many of whom faced or will face incarceration and sentencing."[60] Compare this DOJ response of over 1000 convictions won by the FBI for their law enforcement on the January 6, 2021 event in Washington D.C., in one city, to the absence of evidence of DOJ enforcement of election laws in thousands of cities all over America in the November 2020 election.

There is an incredible void of federal convictions for election law violations. This means there is a lack of enforcement of election laws in states where there is corruption. Most American media sources reported the lack of substantial problems with the 2020 election, but what they don't tell is that there was a lack of federal prosecution of election law violations.

Prosecutors have discretion, which means specifically that federal prosecutors have discretion to prosecute cases, or not. What they prosecute is determined by their leadership. When there is no prosecution of election laws it appears to the nation that there is no evidence of major problems in the election. As we just described, in reality there was little to no federal enforcement of election laws in the November 2020 election. The Heritage Foundation has an active "sampling of recent election fraud cases from across the United States," showing convictions that span over 10 years by state governments, but we again find a void of evidence of federal enforcement—which should be actively found in states not enforcing their election laws.[61] Where there is corruption in a corrupt state, and no federal enforcement of election laws, what can we expect in the future? If there is no law enforcement, will there not continue to be law-breaking?

If the F.B.I. is not enforcing U.S. election laws, how do we know that a government designed to be "of the people, by the people, for the people" is not a government "of the few in power, by the few in power, for the few in power?" We want local law-enforcement officers to be accountable to ensure that local crimes are fairly prosecuted for the safety of our communities. Must we not also demand that our top federal law-enforcement agencies be accountable to assure our fundamental right to vote is not lost?

There is also evidence that big tech companies may be purposely undermining our free and fair election process.

From one researcher: "In 2020, the 1.5 million ephemeral experiences we aggregated from the computers of our 1,735 field agents showed us manipulations that were sufficient, in theory, to have shifted more than six million votes to Joe Biden (who the researcher supported)—again, without people knowing they were being manipulated. Among other findings: Google was sending more go-vote reminders to liberals and moderates than to conservatives; that's a brazen and powerful manipulation that would go completely undetected unless someone was monitoring."[62] This level of election tampering has been intentional and violates not only our election laws, but it also violates federal laws against sedition. Enforcement of these laws against our tech giants by our Department of Justice is scarce.

The FBI has actively used heavy-handed enforcement tactics to come after pro-life Christians, as they did in September of 2022 when they went to the Mark Houck family's home. Mark has been acquitted of the charges against him, but his wife reported of his arrest that a team "of about 25 came to my house with about 15 vehicles and started pounding on our door. They said they were going to break it in if he didn't open it. And then they had about five guns pointed at my husband, myself, and basically at my kids."[63]

The DOJ has also been known for going after parents who want to speak out against the government at local school board meetings. In a report in October of 2021, "a Virginia mother said federal agents infiltrated her local school board meeting after she and other parents protested the Department of Justice for asking the FBI to go after people who disrupt school board meetings."[64]

We now are also finding out that the FBI has known of the Biden family's corruption for years, but, again, with their prosecutorial discretion, they have purposely not prosecuted the Bidens. According to a recent report given by Senator Chuck Grassley, "Based on the information provided to my office over a period of years by multiple credible whistleblowers, there appears to be an effort within the Justice Department and FBI to shut down investigative activity relating to the Biden family. Such decisions point to significant political bias infecting the decision-making of not only the Attorney General and FBI Director, but also line agents and prosecutors."[65] "More than 40 confidential sources provided 'criminal information' related to the Biden family to the FBI—which the Justice Department tried to discredit as 'foreign disinformation,' according to …Grassley."[66]

Why would the FBI not prosecute the Biden family for self-rewarding crimes and corruption that endanger our government's international credibility? Could it be so that Democrats win elections and continue the political agenda and big budgets of Democrats in senior leadership positions in the DOJ? And did the FBI continue to tip the scale against the Republicans by using their prosecutorial discretion to file charges against Donald Trump for alleged mishandling of classified information, while nothing was done for Biden's mishandling of classified material?[67]

Integrity First Answer: If the DOJ Has Become Politically Corrupt, the US Congress Should be Actively Holding Senior Leadership Accountable Through Oversight and Impeachment

As with the U.S. Military, as with the Department of Homeland Security, as with any executive branch involved in corruption and criminal activity, the only branch that can correct this criminal conduct of the U.S. Department of Justice is the U.S. Congress. If there is criminal conduct within the DOJ there is not another law enforcement agency above them. A case may be brought and appealed to the U.S. Supreme Court and the Supreme Court could hold that activity within the DOJ is unlawful, but if the executive branch is corrupt, who will bring the case, and who would enforce a ruling adverse to the DOJ?

Our US Attorney General is responsible for the Department of Justice. If the leadership of the DOJ has become the political puppet of the Democratic Party, and is committing high crimes in favoring one party over another, "Houston, we have a problem!"

The integrity first answer is for the U.S. Congress to impeach the Attorney General and other senior DOJ leaders for the disgraceful high crime of targeting and entrapping political enemies of the party in power. This behavior is how tyrannical governments destroy those that oppose their political positions. As with any city, or county, or state, we also want our federal law enforcement professionals to enforce the laws without bias. If our federal level DOJ is clearly coming after people primarily from one political party, accusing them of crimes of the DOJ's choosing, while they refuse to enforce serious crimes of treason and bribery from those in the party that lead executive agencies, we have a department of injustice, not a Department of Justice. The Congress must exercise strong leadership to rid our executive branch of leaders with bias accompanied by impeachable conduct.

As to U.S. elections, state and federal government law enforcement agencies must enforce our election laws, and we must ensure that we have people in government who will do their jobs in this arena. The Congress must impeach leaders committing high crimes, and ensure through congressional oversight, confirmation powers, and budgeting powers that good leaders are placed in leadership. The DOJ enforcement work must also include going after the election tampering and sedition found in big tech companies that are purposely controlling information to benefit one political party over another. If current DOJ leadership is not doing their job the Congress must see to their replacement by those public servants who will enforce U.S. laws.

If one political party controls the prosecutors in the few key battleground cities and states needed to win national elections they may be able to manipulate and break election laws and change election numbers in every way conceivable, with no fear of prosecution. In this way they can assure themselves of getting just enough votes to make it look close but still win. The integrity first answer is to assure that local, state, and federal prosecutors are doing their job enforcing election laws. Otherwise there is no fear of prosecution for those breaking the laws and a party in power can control battleground cities and states to win federal elections.

We want our local law enforcement professionals to keep us safe from dangerous criminals. We also want our federal law enforcement professionals to keep us safe from dangerous criminals at the federal levels. Our Congress must be active in oversight, and through legal processes it must replace those senior leaders not serving with integrity, including the use of impeachment to dismiss top executive branch officers involved in treason, bribery and other high crimes. We must clean up our federal law enforcement agencies at the top levels, so those serving at all levels under them can serve with honor and integrity.

We need leaders with strong moral courage, who, even in a time of great division in America will take the side of truth and integrity, leading the United States to unity in what is morally good and right. Do we insist that our Congress use its powers of impeachment, oversight, confirmation, and the power of the purse to change the leadership of the DOJ from a culture of political bias to a culture of responsible law enforcement? Do we unify in what is true and right, or do we stay divided in support of corruption and non-enforcement of U.S. laws?

Chapter 10 United States Energy Policy

"There is a way that seems right to a man, but in the end it leads to death." Proverbs 16:25

Intelligence Brief: U.S. Energy Policy from 2021-2024 Strengthened Russia, China, Iran, HAMAS and Other U.S. Enemies

When President Biden took office in January of 2021, he immediately began implementing policies that weakened what had been U.S. oil industry success and national stability. In doing so, he created a domino effect that emboldened the Russians to attack Ukraine, Iran to pour more money into HAMAS and other terrorist organizations, and China to become a greater threat to Taiwan and the U.S. This is another clear example of the "fallacy of the Civil War South"—an obsession on one position leading to blindness to an opposing position. For the Biden Administration there was an emphasis on environmentalism that had falsely concluded that the world would soon be ruined if major changes in energy policy did happen in a very short time frame. This single-mindedness resulted in an inability to see the chain of events that caused major international instability, including two wars (in Ukraine and Israel).

On President Biden's first day in office, he signed numerous executive orders to counter the prior policies of the previous President. One of these was the revocation of the permit for the Keystone XL pipeline. "With the stroke of a pen, Biden canceled a project that would have boosted U.S. gross domestic product by more than $3 billion, carried 830,000 barrels of oil daily from Canada to the United 'states, and directly provided up to 26,000 jobs—11,000 of which were instantly lost."[68] Of course these orders were given glowing environmental names, like Order 13990 (January 20, 2021), "Protecting Public Health and the Environment and Restoring Science To Tackle the Climate Crisis." Buried in this Executive Order, in Section 4, is the "….moratorium on all activities of the Federal Government relating to the implementation of the Coastal Plain Oil and Gas Leasing Program.."[69] These orders included the "…withdrawal of certain offshore areas in Arctic waters and the Bering Sea from oil and gas drilling…"[70] These orders have prevented oil industry development and expansion, and have decreased the ability of the U.S. to be a net exporter of oil and gas.

Just in case there is a question of whether or not President Biden was purposely shifting to a position that emphasized climate policies, in Section 6 of Executive Order 13990, which revoked the permit for the Keystone XL Pipeline, the order states: "Leaving the Keystone XL pipeline permit in place would not be consistent with my Administration's economic and climate imperatives."[71] For Biden, this was all about shifting the economy to reliance on "clean energy" (as his administration described it), and controlling the climate. The United States already has much cleaner emissions standards than other industrial nations. For example, in 2018 China, the world's top emitter, was producing 28 percent of all emissions, compared to just 15% in the United States.[72] "The Asian giant produces more than a quarter of global greenhouse gases, emitting nearly as much as Canada, Europe, and the United States

Combined."[73] China is the one supposedly taking the lead in world climate control, developing and selling electric car technology to support the electric car industry worldwide while they are the worst offenders of dirty emissions.[74]

Regardless of the destabilizing effect on Europe and the Mideast the Biden Administration pushed ahead with its obsession on the climate. President Biden signed an executive order returning the U.S. to the Paris climate accords, and by limiting leases on public lands or offshore waters put in place goals for the U.S. to have net-zero emissions by 2050.[75] As a direct result of these and other executive orders Russia and Iran became dominant suppliers of oil to Europe and other countries that have been U.S. allies.

Because European countries became dependent on Russian oil, they were no longer in a position of strength to counter Russia's attack on Ukraine. Instead of being a dominant independent force to stand strong against Russia's desire to take Ukraine, Europe could not afford to cut economic ties with Russia, because they were depending on Russian oil. While they were trying to support Ukraine in their own feeble ways, Europe could not take a strong stance against Russia because they needed her oil. In the process of buying Russian oil Europe has been funding the Russian military machine that is using its power to take over what had been a free and independent country in Europe. Had Europe been able to rely on U.S. oil supplies, they would have been in a strong position to deter Russian aggression. With Europe dependent on Russian oil, Russia had the confidence to go ahead with its attack on Ukraine.

In Chapter 8 the facts were clearly exposed that the failure of the U.S. to enforce sanctions against Iran's oil industry has allowed them to make millions upon millions of dollars. This great wealth has been used to fund the terrorist organizations that have actively been fighting against Israel, taking U.S. citizens captive, killing them while in captivity, and attacking U.S. forces in the region. The energy policies of the Biden administration are allowing Iran to become very wealthy. Their wealth is being used to fund terrorism, and it is this terrorism that has led to war in the Mideast, which has included the killing of Americans.

Integrity First Answer: The President Should Honor Energy Policy that Keeps U.S. Oil and Gas Industries Strong and Dominant in the World Market

Our U.S. President should not interfere with private development and expansion of U.S oil and gas companies. The Congress is in a position to make laws to protect our environment, which they have done to a level that is much more responsible than most countries. For example, U.S. environmental laws are clearly more environmentally friendly than China's—which is another reason we don't need China leading international efforts that champion a clean environment.

When U.S. oil and natural gas companies are thriving, U.S. gas prices are lower, and the U.S. has greater opportunities to be a supplier of energy in foreign markets. When gas prices are lower, the price of everything that needs to be transported on U.S. highways is also lowered. Greater supply and lower prices of U.S. oil and gas also allow nations that are our allies to trade actively with the U.S. instead of relying on Russia, Iran, and other countries that have shown themselves to be dangerous to the U.S. and to the world.

If European countries are able to benefit from U.S. oil and gas, they can become less dependent on Russia and Iran. This would allow them to join the U.S. in sharing the proper burden to defeat Russian and Iranian expansion. This would be a major help to America's opportunity to lead from a "peace through strength" position. As much as we want to continue to actively use diplomacy and economic policies, many of our main enemies still make their major decisions on power projection. Our energy policy has a direct impact on the United States economically, but also on our either being a powerful nation that leads through strength, or as a weak nation that is unable to deter violence and war.

Chapter 11: Impeachment

"A wicked man accepts a bribe in secret to pervert the course of justice." Proverbs 17:23

Intelligence Brief: Treason, Bribery, and High Crimes

Since taking office early in 2021 President Biden signed many executive orders and made many policy decisions that raise questions of integrity. If a strong case can be made that many decisions he made were deceitful, dangerous, and criminal, then we have integrity problems. Several decisions of President Biden that could have been considered impeachable conduct are outlined in this chapter. But we first respond to those who are against impeaching Presidents because they fear we are encouraging a precedent of mere political retribution.

Far too many politicians wanted to argue that impeaching President Biden would have set a bad precedent for Congress because it would have set a pattern of impeaching a President for political reasons. The first and primary problem with this is that the reasons for impeachment should not be based on politics, but on whether a president is committing crimes dangerous to the American people. We all have elected prosecutors in our local areas, and we expect them to have the integrity to do their jobs and go after dangerous criminals. We don't want them to sit around and make political excuses for not prosecuting the dangerous criminals. If the President is committing treason, accepting bribes, or other high crimes dangerous to our country, then he should be impeached before he does more damage. If there is integrity in the decision to impeach, it is about the truth of the facts that show treason, bribery, or other high crimes (U.S. Const., Art. 2, Sec. 4). Impeaching a president is not about a party playing political games, it's about our Congress doing their job to prosecute dangerous criminal conduct.

Another important way to analyze this is to observe that the impeachment of Donald Trump by the Democrats actually was motivated by partisan politics, but this should not end the use of impeachment when we do find dangerous, impeachable conduct in the future. The Democrats impeachment of Trump demonstrated the wastefulness and wrongness of impeachment for political reasons. The impeachment cases argued by the Democrats were high on rhetoric and disdain for Trump but lacked facts and evidence to support their charges. The fact that one party abused the impeachment process for their own political agenda was clear for all to see, and should not negate the duty of the Congress to impeach a current president who is committing treason, bribery, or other high crimes dangerous to our nation.

If the President of the United States has integrity, he will not be committing treason, bribery, and other high crimes dangerous to the peace and security of the United States. If we have a Congress that has integrity they will impeach a President, and any other top executive officers in government, for acts of treason, taking bribes from foreign nations, or other high crimes dangerous to our nation.

Any one of the following fact patterns is a valid reason for impeachment:

Failure to Enforce our Immigration Laws and to Secure Our Borders

The treasonous and deadly failure to enforce our immigration laws and to secure our borders are impeachable offenses. The evidence of these dangerous crimes was reviewed in Chapter 3. This failure to secure our nation's borders is evidenced by millions who have illegally been allowed into our country. These include terrorists, sex-slave traders, dangerous gangs, enemies of the U.S., and drug dealers (including sellers of deadly drugs like fentanyl), all sharing a common purpose to destroy the lives of Americans.

Hasty Surrender and Withdrawal from Afghanistan

The treasonous decision to quickly withdraw from Afghanistan, giving back to the enemy all that was gained by the blood and sacrifice of Americans, arming our enemies with massive amounts of military equipment, and returning the Taliban and their terrorist agents to full power were impeachable offenses. (See chapter 6)

Failure to Intercept and Destroy the Chinese Spy Balloon Before It Flew Across the U.S.

To allow an unknown aircraft to fly across the U.S. was a treasonous failure to protect the United States, aiding an enemy in their free flight of a large, guided balloon, whose contents were unknown until it fully passed over many important military bases. Only after it traveled across the U.S. was it shot down and the contents were identified as Chinese (spy) surveillance equipment. An aircraft from an enemy nation heading toward the U.S. should have been intercepted and evaluated before it reached North American airspace, and either turned away, or if it failed to identify its purpose and change course, it should have been destroyed before it reached U.S. shores. (See chapter 7).

The Use of the U.S. DOJ to Further Biden's Political Agenda

The high crimes committed in the misuse of power by President Biden using the Department of Justice to further his own political agenda are impeachable offenses. (See chapter 9)

The Biden Family Receiving Bribes

Evidence has become clear that from the time Joe Biden was the U.S. Vice President the Biden family has received millions of dollars from foreign governments, including China and Ukraine.[76] As to whether all money improperly received must be specifically received individually by Joe Biden for it to be criminal, "the law recognizes payment to family members to corruptly influence others can constitute a bribe."[77] Another example of this bribery is from a FBI informant file "describing a $10 million bribery allegation against President Biden and his son Hunter

.....showing that a Ukrainian oligarch claimed that he was 'coerced' into making the payoff."[78]

Funding of Iran with U.S. Dollars

It is treason for the U.S. to put $6 Billion in the hands of Iran, one the world's largest supporters of terrorism and thus clearly our enemy, while negotiating with terrorists in a "deal" to release 5 Iranian prisoners for 5 American prisoners.[79] The U.S. failure to take a strong stance against Iran has allowed Iran to fund terrorist organizations like HAMAS, which executed the horrific terrorist attack in Israel against Israeli and American women, children, and men. (See Chapter 8)

The Integrity First Answer: Impeach Top Executive Branch Leaders Who Commit Crimes Against the United States

When we have dangerous criminals in cities, we require that our police chiefs do their job: arrest and prosecute the criminals for their dangerous crimes. There would be no integrity in a police chief to conclude that because he cannot trust the jury to do their job, he is not going to do his job in bringing a criminal to trial. This same is true of our House and Senate when they refuse to Impeach a President and Vice President because they think the Senate is too politically weak to honor the facts and the law.

According to the U.S. Constitution Congress is in the role of the prosecutor when the President, Vice President and other top executive branch officers are committing dangerous criminal activity. The U.S. House of Representatives brings articles of impeachment, and the U.S. Senate conducts the trial. If our U.S. Congress had integrity, they should have been actively impeaching numerous top U.S. officials, including President Biden, and Vice President Harris, for the impeachable offenses listed above. Prosecutors all over America are in the daily conduct of pursuing multiple criminal prosecutions. Our U.S. Congress should have been doing the same.

We have had clear evidence of treason, bribery and other high crimes, clearly impeachable offenses according to Article 2, Section 4 of the U.S. Constitution. As an Air Force Academy cadet we had an honor code that we lived under, that we would not lie, cheat, or steal, or tolerate anyone who violated these standards. There is no honor in committing treason, bribery and other high crimes, but there is also no honor in tolerating these crimes.

Every member of Congress, Democrat, Republican, or Independent should be leading the charge to impeach and dismiss any President or Vice President committing treason, bribery, or other high crimes. Congress should have the integrity to not tolerate this dangerous criminal conduct, and to do the job they committed to do when they took their oath, and hold our top executives accountable for treason, bribery, and other high crimes. Each day they fail to impeach dangerous criminals in top leadership positions in the executive branch is another day of more criminal activity being committed by dangerous senior officials who remain in their jobs.

The Integrity First Answer would be to impeach any President, Vice President, or other top executive branch leaders who have committed treason, bribery, and other high crimes. It is the right thing to do. And, as is usually the case, the right thing to do is the more difficult thing to do—these tasks have apparently been too difficult for our U.S. Congresses over the last few years. Without correcting the executive branch's bad leadership, the United States risks a continuous headlong fall into weakness, debt, and decline.

What is strong moral leadership? Even in a time of great division, the integrity first Answer is to take the side of truth and justice, leading to unity in what is morally good and right. Leaders in Congress have made the decision day after day to not impeach our dangerous senior leadership—to tolerate treason, bribery, and other high crimes at the top of our executive branch of government. Do we unify in what is true and right correcting criminal conduct, or do we stay divided in support of dangerous criminal conduct?

Chapter 12: What is a Woman?

"Haven't you read," he replied, "that at the beginning the Creator made them male and female..." (Jesus) Matthew 19:4

Intelligence Brief: Women, Men and a State of Mind

Many people in the United States have been trained to think that it is "hate speech" whenever you say something that may offend someone. Any good parent knows this is not the case. When a child says they want to be the boss and they want to be in charge of the day's activities, good parents let the child know they are not the boss, and the child will not be running things. It is actually "love speech" when a child is trained about what is true and false, and what is right and wrong—even if it offends them at the time.

If a child says they want to go through physical surgeries so they can be a cat, or to change from being a girl to a boy, or a boy to a girl, it is "love speech" to be honest with them and let them know the truth. That a child is not a cat. A boy is not a girl. A girl is not a boy. A person can act like they are something they are not—they can have mental thoughts about being something they are not—we call that imagination, or acting, or some other description of one's state of mind.

If we love children, we must be honest with them, and let them know how dangerous it is to go through medical treatment and surgeries that mutilate their bodies and can render them unable to have children, or nurse children, or have other health problems that will remain with them the rest of their lives, just because of thoughts they are having in their minds. If a child is asking to go through such drastic procedures, what needs time and attention is not what is going on with their healthy bodies that are still developing—and that may be going through the healthy natural process of puberty. What needs time and attention is what is going on in their minds. They need to be told the truth that no matter what drugs they may take or what surgeries they go through, the cells in their bodies and minds are either male or female and this cannot be changed with drugs or surgeries.[80] People can pretend to be someone they are not, they can go through medical surgeries to appear like something they are not, but the cells that dominate their bodies and minds are either male or female.

For a man to genuinely go around acting like he is a woman, or to behave as if he can become the amazing human being that women are designed to be, is an insult to women. Consider a man who wants to compete on a women's NCAA gymnastics team, or another women's team of your choice. Those of us who think logically and honestly know that a man who tries to compete with women, as if he were a woman, with the qualities and mannerisms of women, is an insult to women. This is not hate speech, this is being honest.

The opposite is also true. For a woman to genuinely go around acting like she is a man, or to behave as if she can become the amazing human being that men are designed to be, is an insult to men. Consider a woman who wants to compete on an NCAA men's football team, or another men's team of your choice. Those of us who think logically and honestly know that a woman who tries to compete with men, as if she were a man, with the qualities and mannerisms of men, is an insult to men. Again, this is not hate speech, this is being honest.

What's more, if we define love as a decision to give someone our attention and to do what is in their best interest, we would not be showing any love for women to put them in a football game, or in a boxing ring or a fight ring, competing against men who we know could do them great bodily injury. Likewise, we would not want men on a girls team to compete against women in a basketball game, or a soccer game, when we know the men's speed and strength could be very dangerous to the women.

We have confused political agendas and mental conditions with the truth. Senator Marsha Blackburn asked Judge Ketanji Brown Jackson during Supreme Court nomination proceedings, "Can you provide a definition for the word 'woman'?" After a brief exchange Jackson said, "No, I can't…. not in this context. I'm not a biologist."[81] This failure to be honest was either from political pressure she was feeling, or the result of years of brainwashing about physical and mental conditions that should be known to anyone with a functioning adult mind. Either way it was an unwillingness to give an honest answer from someone who is now a U.S. Supreme Court Justice. The truth is that a woman can be defined as a person with XX chromosomes in the cells of their body and who was born with female sex organs designed to allow the woman to become pregnant and bear children. Women are not men, and men are not women.

For those who fear suicidal tendencies, the greatest suicidal danger is in those who go through sex change operations. From a 30 year follow-up study conducted in Sweden, a culture strongly supportive of such behavior, "Ten to 15 years after surgical reassignment, the suicide rate of those who had undergone sex-reassignment surgery rose to 20 times that of comparable peers."[82] If we love people who are struggling with these mental issues, we are not showing them any love and compassion by encouraging them to go down such a dangerous road.

Integrity First Answer: Those Considering Sex-Reassignment Surgery Should Be Informed They Cannot Change the Gender of Each Cell in Their Bodies, and It Is Criminal Child Abuse and Mutilation for Children to Go Through Sex Change Procedures

The truth is that men and women are different. They are designed differently. It is a lie to tell a woman that she can become a man, or to tell a man he can become a woman. Men and women can mentally believe that they are the opposite sex, but their belief does not change the physical make-up of the cells in their bodies. Each individual cell in our bodies is unchangeably either male or female. No drug therapy or surgery can change the chemical structure of each human cell. We show greater love to people to tell them of this truth than to advance and tolerate a dangerous lie.

If adults want to knowingly make a mental decision to live their lives as something they physically are not, they have that freedom in our current society, but it should be an informed decision, when they are legally old enough to make such life-altering choices. It is of great importance that we be honest with people we love and be sure they know of the risks and dangers inherent in taking drugs and having surgeries that are not healthy considering the way a body is designed as male or female. The obvious risks include the destruction of otherwise healthy reproductive systems, negative impacts on other physiological systems, and higher rates of mental problems that can end in suicide.

As to children, those under the age of 18, it is criminal child abuse and mutilation of children to allow them to go through life altering medical treatment that destroys healthy reproductive systems. Children are unable to make informed decisions because of their physiological and psychological underdevelopment, and they are subject to frequent changes in the decisions they make on any topic. Even college-age students frequently change their minds about the careers they want to pursue, the friends they make, the people they date, and even whether they want to have a family or not. How dangerous it would be to allow a child younger than college age to make life-changing decisions that could render them sterile and unable to have their own children with a future spouse they have yet to meet. Children are too young to appreciate the dangers of taking drugs and having surgeries that remove sexual organs. And they may be unable to comprehend that the cell structure of every part of the body and the brain cannot be changed from male to female, or female to male. Even though they think they want a physical transformation it is truthfully not possible, and they should be told the truth.

Though we have laws in some states against the abuse and mutilation of children that occur in transgender surgeries, other states debate penalizing parents for not allowing these surgeries, and some are fighting to allow children to make transgender transition decisions independent of the influence of their parents.[83] Parents must be active and informed about the laws that may be changing in their states, and make every effort to protect their children from dangerous laws that may allow such criminal abuse and mutilation of their children.[84]

What is the leadership of Lincoln? In a time of great division, we should take the side of truth and integrity, leading to unity in what is morally good and right. The truth is that, physically, women are women and men are men. People can make mental decisions to live various lifestyles, but they should be informed that they cannot change the cell structure of each cell of their body which is either male or female. Children should not be manipulated into the criminal mutilation of their bodies by lies they are told; that they can become boys when they are girls, or they can become girls when they are boys. Laws should be passed to protect our children from these dangerous medical procedures. Do we unify in what is true and right to protect our children, or do we stay divided in support of lies and child abuse?

Chapter 13: Corporate America and International Trade

"The Bible says somewhere that we are desperately selfish. I think we would have discovered that fact without the Bible."[85] *Abraham Lincoln*

Intelligence Brief: America Sacrifices Integrity for Profit

When corporate America wants to minimize their labor costs, they go to other nations where they can find cheap labor.[86] These corporate leaders claim to have compassion for everyone. The truth is they have little concern for the ongoing human rights violations in countries like China. They know that in the countries they go to for cheap labor there is an absence of protections for workers that U.S. laws provide—protections like workers compensation laws, minimum wage, laws against child labor and unreasonably long work hours. They would rather go to countries with massive human rights problems where people will work for a fraction of what is required in the United States. Their priority is not integrity but profit. It's a similar breach of integrity as what we faced in the South at the time of slavery, where men prioritized profit over morality.

Capitalism in America allows for great opportunities for individuals and corporations to compete and become very wealthy. Marxism considers this dangerous because it claims that the wealthy will take advantage of the poor. In the United States we have laws that protect workers, and attorneys that are very willing to sue corporations and their leaders when they break labor laws and take advantage of workers. In communist countries and other tyrannical governments they don't have these laws to protect the rights of individuals, or the attorneys with the freedom to go after those in power. What they do have are governments that control, own, and benefit from the companies and labor that are in their countries.

In communist countries, not only is there a loss of freedom, but there is a loss of excellence. With a lack of competition comes a lack of high quality. Why do we not buy Chinese cars in America—or Russian cars? They have not produced the quality that comes from active competition. This has been changing some as U.S. companies contractually require more quality from Chinese products to meet U.S. standards. But you will not find in China successful independent companies like Ford, or General Motors, as the Chinese government has joint ownership in their companies, and their doctrine does not allow independent corporate power that could rise up to rival the government's power—because the government in communist countries is determined to control everything.

When U.S. companies work with foreign companies in communist countries and use foreign labor to produce goods, the money paid to these foreign companies supports their tyrannical governments. The U.S. has made communist China very wealthy. With this wealth China is constantly increasing the strength of its military so it can challenge the U.S. on the world stage.[87] Meanwhile China uses every tool at its disposal, including social media such as Tik Tok, to damage the U.S.[88] If you have any doubt that China is our enemy just consider how much death and destruction they caused in the United States when they released COVID in America, killing thousands of Americans, and doing great harm to our economy.

Why do Americans buy so many products made in China, supporting a Chinese communist government? America does not prioritize integrity, they prioritize what is practical—what can save them money. Americans would rather pay lower prices for clothes, and shoes, and computers, and cell phones, etc., than have to pay a higher price for goods made in the U.S., or in other free countries.

Another example of compromising integrity for monetary gain is how the U.S. has encouraged companies like Gotion Inc., a company owned and controlled by China's Gotion High-Tech, to build electric battery plants in the U.S., operating as a U.S. sanctioned entity in a joint venture with the People's Republic of China (PRC).[89] The temptation for U.S. communities to cooperate with the Chinese is immense, as demonstrated by Gotion Inc.'s approval from Michigan Democrat Governor Gretchen Whitmer and the Biden administration "to 'invest $2.4 billion to construct two 550,000-square-foot production plants' for electric (EV) batteries in Big Rapids, Michigan."[90] The state of Illinois has also recently announced that Gotion Inc. intends to "build a 'state-of-the-art $2 billion' EV battery plant in Manteno, Illinois, 'bolstered' by state incentives."[91] This may bring billions of dollars into these U.S. communities, but who is ultimately benefiting from this corporate activity? China is getting rich from American markets.

If the immorality of dealing with the Chinese is not obvious, here is more detail. China's Gotion High-Tech, the parent company of Gotion, Inc. has a joint investment relationship with the Shanghai Electric Group, Ltd., establishing Shanghai Electric Gotion New Energy

Technology Co., Ltd.—which is operating a "battery energy storage system for a Xinjiang Production and Construction Corps (XPCC) power station located in China's Xinjiang Uyghur Autonomous Region (XUAR).[92] "The XPCC is a paramilitary organization in the XUAR that is subordinate to the Chinese Communist Party (CCP)," and has been sanctioned by the U.S. Treasury Department, for its human rights abuses.[93]

You may have heard of the atrocities in the XUAR (Uyghur), but more detail is found in the following 2022 State Department's Country Report on Human Rights:

"Genocide and crimes against humanity occurred during the year against predominantly Muslim Uyghurs and members of other ethnic and religious minority groups in Xinjiang. These crimes were continuing and included: the arbitrary imprisonment or other severe deprivation of physical liberty of more than one million civilians; forced sterilization, coerced abortions and more restrictive application of the country's birth control policies; rape and other forms of sexual and gender-based violence; torture of a large number of those arbitrarily detained; and persecution including forced labor and draconian restrictions on freedom of religion or belief, freedom of expression and freedom of movement."[94]

This is what happened in Nazi Germany. This is what happens in communist countries where there is absolute control of a country from a federal government that controls everything. They can carry out genocide and there is no one there to hold them accountable. Hopefully the states that are planning for these Chinese plants to come to America will change their minds, but why do U.S. companies even consider such economic relationships with China? They do it for the money. Why do we buy anything from

China? We know the answer, it's because Americans prioritize low prices over morality and integrity.

There actually have been a couple of situations in America where foolish corporate decision-making has resulted in American consumers boycotting big companies, impacting corporate profits. Disney came out very strong against Florida's parental rights law in March of 2022, resulting in numerous families boycotting Disney. In an August 2023 report Disney's financial reports showed, "the company's market cap has fallen from $350.09 billion on March 22, 2022, to $154.04 billion. That's a decline of $196.05 billion—or a 56% drop."[95]   A second example is when Bud Light used transgender influencer Dylan Mulvaney, and Anheuser-Busch InBev reported "that revenue in the United States declined by 10.5% in the April-to-June period from a year earlier, 'primarily due to the volume decline of Bud Light.' "[96]   There may be hope that American consumers are taking more of a stand on moral issues by how they spend their money.

Another reason for Americans to hold corporations accountable for their outsourcing of jobs to foreign countries like China is the failure of many of these countries to meet the environmental safety standards of the U.S.[97] Those who are genuinely concerned about the environment should stop buying products from countries that have not taken the environmental safety precautions taken in the United States.

As was discussed in Chapter 9, the U.S. Department of Justice is not actively enforcing the blatant tampering in elections that has been coming from social media giants like Google and Facebook. Google has been actively favoring speech that promotes liberal Democrat Party candidates, but opposing the speech that could be helpful to conservative Republicans.[98] Facebook's (rebranded Meta in 2021) founder and CEO, Mark Zuckerberg is now famous for his "Zuckerbucks" or "Zuck Bucks," giving millions of dollars to battleground cities like Chicago and Philadelphia, where he "provided new election infrastructure critical to Joe Biden's victory over President Donald Trump," and allowed for "an unprecedented flood of largely untraceable, potentially fraudulent mail-in ballots submitted via private drop-boxes with no official oversight or accountability."[99] Yet U.S. conservatives continue to actively use Google and Facebook, supporting these companies and their billionaire leaders who are determined to single-handedly control our election results—if nothing else than by controlling the information flow on their media platforms.

Integrity First Answer: American Consumers Should Stop Doing Business with Corporations that Lack Integrity and Corporations Tampering with U.S. Elections Should be Prosecuted

U.S. consumers have the opportunity to stop buying products from companies that outsource production and stop buying products made in countries that violate people's human rights. Americans should pay attention to where products they are buying are made and stop making tyrannical governments like China wealthy. Otherwise, we continue to make our enemies more powerful while they continue to deprive their people of many of the basic human rights we take for granted.

U.S. consumers should also stop supporting American companies like Google and Facebook (Meta) that have facilitated active tampering in U.S. elections. When we know these companies are actively manipulating political speech and financing tactics that give great advantage to political liberals, why are most political conservatives still using Google and Facebook? This is another example of when doing the right thing is the more difficult thing, but most Americans don't want to be inconvenienced. The Integrity First Answer would be for conservative Americans to stop using these social media platforms that have provided such wealth to those who aggressively and actively oppose conservative candidates and policies.

American leaders in private corporations and in government should stop contracting with foreign companies known for their human rights violations and environmental recklessness. U.S. sanctions against these countries should be enforced. Our federal, state, and local governments should not be working and contracting with private and foreign companies in countries like China. In doing so, we are making them stronger and enabling them to take advantage of their own citizens, while planning to do us harm.

U.S. or foreign companies that are actively working to interfere with U.S. elections should be prosecuted by the U.S. Department of Justice. If there is no enforcement of U.S. election laws, there will continue to be election law violations that go unnoticed and uncorrected, compromising U.S. election results.

Does the United States have any leaders like Lincoln out there who will stand up for what is true and right, even though it may be costly? American corporations should have the integrity to stop using foreign labor in countries that violate people's human rights. American companies should not be actively engaged in business contracts and arrangements that are making tyrannical governments like China, Russia, and Iran, more wealthy and powerful. U.S. consumers should take a stand and not buy goods from countries determined to harm us, nor support corporations who enable unethical partisan use of their products to manipulate information and even election results to advance their political agendas.

Chapter 14: Women in Combat

"The glory of young men is their strength, gray hair the splendor of the old." Proverbs 20:29

Intelligence Brief: There Is Not a Women's Section and a Men's Section in Combat

Combat in the military may be very high tech, but anyone with experience in combat knows it can also quickly become very physical. This is why all of our military branches have physical requirements. While each branch of the military has hundreds of jobs that do not require the level of physical challenges involved in hand-to-hand combat, each branch also has complex combat jobs requiring the highest levels of physical conditioning. We should want service members trained and ready for physical combat who have top levels of speed, strength, and stamina, ready to face the most dangerous of enemies.

Women have served actively in and around combat in every war fought by the U.S. since the Revolutionary War.[100] Women have been willing to serve in the most dangerous of combat situations. This is not a question of whether women have served bravely in combat. They have served bravely and they have served well. This is not a question of whether women are capable of serving in combat. The question is whether women should serve in what can become the most intense of physical challenges known to mankind—is it right? Do we want the most capable fighting units to be fighting our nation's wars? If we want the best teams we can put on the field to fight our wars, should they include women?

The door opened up for women to officially serve in combat roles in the U.S. military through a series of executive branch orders, such as the policy put in place in 2015 by then Secretary of Defense Ashton Carter. He decided "that the military would be opening all 'remaining occupations and positions' to women, there will be no exceptions."[101] But who should make such a decision?

The U.S. Supreme Court has dealt with the question of who should be making such policy pertaining to women in the military, and has held that these types of decisions are clearly under the powers of the U.S. Congress, and that "the constitutional power of Congress to raise and support armies and to make all laws necessary and proper to that end is broad and sweeping."[102] While this case did not deal specifically with women in combat, it held that it was not a violation of the equal protection clause for the Congress to decide that registration for the draft should be limited to men. The case makes clear that decisions regarding men and women in the military are decisions that should be made by Congress, not by one person in the executive branch acting as if they alone have the power to make important decisions involving women's roles in the military.

If we understand that there are many combat roles in military service that can become very physical, and if we want the most capable military service members to fight in our wars, the question comes down to whether or not women in these roles give us the most capable fighting units. Three basic arguments of fact are presented to answer this question.

First, it has become clear in women's sports that it is not fair or safe for women to compete against men.[103] We would not want to see a woman fighting a man in a boxing ring, or in a fight ring. This would be abusive to women, dangerous to women, and unacceptable. There are some women very willing to enter this arena against men, but this doesn't make it good or right.

Second, when considering men's NCAA basketball, it is clear that men competing on men's teams are faster, stronger, and have more stamina in their competitions than women. If it was required that two women play on a men's team of five against other teams with all men, it would clearly be unfair, an insult, and demoralizing to the men that they should try to win with two women on their team when the other teams are allowed to have all men. The best NCAA basketball teams are teams with all men.

Third, when considering men's NCAA football, it is clear that men competing on men's teams are faster, stronger, and have more stamina in their competitions than women. If it was required that 4 women play on a team of 11 against other teams with all men, it would clearly be unfair, an insult, and demoralizing to the men that they should try to win with 4 women on their team when the other teams are allowed to have all men. The best NCAA football teams are teams with all men.

In physical military combat, there will not be a men's section and a women's section. All will be fighting on the same field, or in the same city, possibly going tree to tree, house to house, in very difficult combat environments. In such difficult, challenging, physical environments, is the best team we can put on this field a team with women, or a team of all men?

The Integrity First Answer: Physical Combat Roles Should Be for Men

Military physical combat can be very demanding. The United States should want the fastest, the strongest, the most physically capable teams trained and ready to go into combat to fight for our freedoms. Since the beginning of time combat has dominantly been carried out by men trained to fight in the most challenging of physical environments. The facts are clear to all, military combat can become very physical. As outlined above it is also clear that men are dominantly more capable of serving in physical combat roles. If we want the best fighting units to fight for our freedom in combat, they should be men. Who should decide this question? As was reviewed in the case law in the previous section, the government body that should make this decision is the U.S. Congress.

The U.S. Congress, as is the case in so many situations, has not taken strong positions in important matters such as this one, but has taken the politically safe position of staying out of socially controversial decisions. The truth is, the question of women's roles as part of our physical combat forces is a clear example of the failure of Congress to be strong and bold in making important and sweeping decisions when such decisions involve politically hot issues and special interest groups fighting over controversial topics. What is needed are strong moral leaders who will make good decisions about what is best for our country, even when doing so will result in strong opposition. Again, this is the leadership of Lincoln—even when half the country opposes you, a leader with integrity and moral courage will fight for what is right, based on the facts.

As this book gets to this final chapter, this question of whether or not women should serve in physical combat is given as a classic example of the current leadership crisis in America. The current policy allowing women in physical combat is an example of a lack of leadership from politicians driven by personal advancement, versus the leadership of Lincoln, who was driven by what was right for our country. The politicians in Congress who refuse to take stands for what is right, and for what most Americans want for the good of the country, instead prioritize what is safest for their political future. They take positions too often that are driven by political acceptance. They fear losing votes from a few voters that may oppose them rather than standing for the truth and winning the support of most voters who will join them.

What we need are leaders who will stand and fight the difficult battles for what is best for America. The United States needs leaders who demand that immigration laws are enforced, the national debt is paid off, human life in a mother's womb is protected, military and civilian leaders guilty of treason are prosecuted, corrupt leaders in the executive branch are impeached, nations come together to defeat HAMAS and other terrorist organizations, children are protected from dangerous misinformation and gender reassignment surgery mutilation, American corporate leaders are stopped from taking advantage of international workers and end their attack on free speech and end their election tampering, and men serve in physical combat roles to fight against other men.

What is needed in America are leaders with moral courage. We need leaders with integrity who honor the truth and who will unite us with good and right decisions, even in times of division when there are strong opposing positions. As we need integrity to have success in the military, we must have integrity in our families, in our churches, in our businesses, in media, in education, and in government—it's an answer to every problem in America. May our trust be in God to help us find leaders with strong moral courage, who put integrity first.

EPILOGUE

In the closing days of writing this book, the conservatives in America have won victories to take back the majority in both branches of Congress, and with Donald Trump they have won back the office of the U.S. President. While this is very exciting for those of us with conservative values and principles, it is yet to be seen if these newly elected officials will have integrity, and will actually lead with strong moral courage, or not.

In the "Integrity First Answer" sections of this book I have suggested leadership remedies to problems Americans are facing. These have been primarily legal remedies. We need leaders with the courage to stand for what is right and who will take the steps necessary to hold bad leaders accountable.

For broader application, as we think ahead, there are three areas where we need U.S. leaders and citizens with strong moral courage. The first area is that of enforcement. The second is that of responsible voting. The final area is that of responsible consumer spending.

As to enforcement. If we live in a community where there is someone breaking into our homes and stealing from us, or a killer on the loose who is attacking and killing people, we want our law enforcement professionals to go and find the criminals, prosecute them, and get them off of our streets. There must be enforcement, or crimes will continue.

The same can be said for those who have committed dangerous crimes in government service. If we have had executive branch leaders who have committed treason, aiding our enemies so those enemies can steal from us, take advantage of us, and kill us, those who have committed these crimes should be held accountable. For example our failure to hold U.S. leaders accountable for their treason in Vietnam and Afghanistan only keeps the door open for future leaders to make the same mistakes. The same can be said of those who have been committing voter fraud and other crimes dangerous to our republic. There should be a day of reckoning for those who have been committing crimes while in public service, including those within the U.S. Military and those within the U.S. Department of Justice, so that this criminal conduct ends.

The second area where we need leaders of strong moral courage is within our nation's voters. We need citizens who are informed about the truth of what is going on in our nation and in our government, and who are willing to end the terms of politicians who have not been strong moral leaders. We need Americans who vote for those who are courageous leaders of principle, rather than weak politicians.

We as voters must be leaders in the information war, and stop using and supporting sources of information that have been misleading us to believe false information. Instead we should be following information sources that allow freedom of information and freedom of speech, so that both sides of any argument can be clearly heard. In an environment of freedom, voters can find the truth, and stand for what is right and good for our nation.

Voters also must stay informed about what their elected members of Congress are voting for and against. A politician can try to convince you they are for cutting the debt, but if they keep voting for temporary budgets that keep spending at current levels with no plan to pay down the debt, they should be voted out of office. A politician can say they are pro-life, but if they end up passing legislation that uses our taxpayer dollars to pay for abortions in our military, they should be voted out of office. We must find and elect leaders who are not just telling us what we want to hear, but who will have the moral courage to end what is evil and do what is right.

A third area where we need leaders with strong moral courage is in our consumer spending. We need to be honest and diligent as we consider who we may be supporting in how we spend our money. For example, we want what is good for the people of China, but we are not helping the Chinese people when we continue to make the leaders of the Chinese Communist Party rich and powerful. The more wealth and power that goes to the Chinese communist leaders the more difficult it becomes for the people to achieve freedom. And in the process of buying goods and services from China, we are funding the massive military build-up of a communist country who wants to defeat us. American consumers should demand that U.S. corporations stop using China to manufacture their goods. We need consumers in America who will be moral and courageous and not buy goods from corporations that are using cheap labor from communist countries.

We also need courageous consumers who will stop supporting the media giants who are using their power and wealth to deceive the American people and keep us from knowing the truth. When Americans actively use media platforms that deceitfully give political advantage to political liberals, then it is these Americans (many of them conservatives) who are creating wealth for corporate leaders who are determined to use their wealth to defeat U.S. conservatism. In this active use of these social media platforms controlled by liberals, Americans en masse are supporting corrupt leaders who are using their power and wealth to support liberal politicians who want to control the government and take away our freedoms. Though it will take moral courage, Americans need to move from media sources that restrict free speech to those sources that allow the free exchange of ideas.

In 2026 we look forward to the opportunity to celebrate 250 years of this experiment in freedom which is ongoing in the United States of America. If we want freedom to continue to ring in this country, and if we want tyranny to end, we must choose leaders with integrity who love truth and freedom; leaders with strong moral courage who will stand for what is right. This can only happen if laws are enforced, voters are responsible and diligent in their search for truth and in their successful election of government leaders with integrity, and if consumers will stop making rich the nations and liberal corporate millionaires and billionaires who are determined to destroy the United States.

We desperately need American leaders who are not just playing political games for selfish gain and who pursue misguided evil policies. We desperately need American leaders who have the strong moral courage to lead with integrity first so America can be good again, strong again, and free again.

Acknowledgments

Many have influenced the development of this book, but special thanks is given here to my two sisters, Laura Bagg and Mariana Eddy who have given active inputs and technical assistance, and to my greatest source of inspiration this side of heaven, my wonderful wife Julie, who has helped me in this endeavor in every way imaginable.

Exhibit A

Declaration of Freedom from Tyranny, July 5, 2023

To secure God given unalienable rights of freedom, including the rights to life, liberty, and the pursuit of happiness, the United States of America founders have created a system of checks and balances, requiring that each branch check the power of the other branches and that the powers of each branch be separate. The behavior of the people as to what is lawful and what is unlawful should be determined by the legislative process. The duty of the executive branch includes primarily the faithful duty to enforce the laws generated by the Congress. When in the conduct of the United States Federal Government's activity it becomes clear that the executive agencies are not enforcing the laws passed by Congress, but instead have taken on tyrannical power and by their action, or inaction, are taking away freedom, security, and life itself from the people, the Congress of the United States, by design in the U.S. Constitution, is the branch that should hold executive branch leadership accountable via oversight, control of the budget, and impeachment for the removal of corrupt and dangerous leadership.

To prove the current tyranny of our United States Executive branch the following facts are submitted to the U.S. Congress for immediate oversight, spending adjustments, and impeachment actions.

The U.S. President, Secretary of Defense, and other top military leaders have committed high crimes against the U.S. in their reckless withdrawal from Afghanistan, by leaving large quantities of U.S. arms in the hands of our adversaries.

The U.S. President, Vice President, Homeland Security Director, and other executive branch leaders have committed high crimes against the U.S. by their willful and reckless failure to enforce U.S. immigration laws thereby allowing millions of people to illegally come into the United States, including terrorists, criminals, slave traders, drug dealers and other enemies of our nation, as well as people with illnesses known to be dangerous to our health.

The U.S. President has committed bribery and other high crimes by accepting millions of dollars from foreign governments with no lawful reason other than to benefit him and his family and to prejudice his own decision-making to give advantage to these other nations.

The U.S. Attorney General and the U.S. Department of Justice senior leadership are guilty of high crimes by their willful and reckless bias in primarily prosecuting their own political enemies while purposely failing to prosecute criminal conduct of the President, the President's family, and others of his party in senior leadership.

While each state has a duty to create laws that ensure fair and efficient elections, a state's government cannot be trusted to enforce those laws when criminal election conduct has resulted in corrupt leaders gaining power. By its own manuals the Federal Department of Justice is the primary government power in a position to enforce election laws and to assure fair and just elections in such situations where state leadership is not enforcing their own election laws. The U.S. Attorney General, and other Department of Justice senior executive leaders, have committed high crimes in their willful and reckless failure to prosecute and enforce election law misconduct, and this has prevented the votes of the people from being counted accurately, denying thousands their right to vote and resulting in corrupt election outcomes.

Tyranny in the current executive branch includes false and biased reporting of facts, improper pressure on private information sources, and failure to give a clear accounting of facts that should be available to the public, and such misrepresentations show clear attempts by the executive branch to unlawfully influence elections, and more fundamentally to tyrannically control the thoughts and minds of the people. This tyranny over the thoughts and minds of the people should be corrected by the Congress conducting active oversight hearings to ensure that facts that should be available to the public are made public, by the Congress removing federal funding from the current National Public Radio system, and by the Congress requiring that private media companies that claim to be sources of news and open dialogue openly allow freedom of speech in the reporting of competing political positions, or clearly identify themselves as political organizations, not news organizations.

Freedom from judicial activism requires that the Congress, not judges, make decisions regarding the behavior of the people as lawful or unlawful, and where the Supreme Court and other judges have entered the arena of law making, the Congress should actively re-enter and make laws regarding public behavior, rather than leaving these decisions to judges.

The federal executive branch should end executive branch orders for federal funding for abortions where no such power has been given by Congress, as such funding is clearly a power of legislative bodies governing human behavior, not the power of the executive branch.

The child in the womb is a human life, and, as any other person, has the right to life, liberty, and the pursuit of happiness. Those who focus on the rights of the mother to the exclusion of the rights of the child make the same moral mistake in history as those who demanded rights for slave owners to the exclusion of the rights of slaves, and history will show their wrong thinking in fighting for abortion as it has shown the wrong thinking of those who fought for slavery. The Congress, the President, and the Courts should unite in proclaiming that in the United States of America, the child in the womb is a human being with the right to life, liberty, and the pursuit of happiness. As with any case where a human life endangers the life of another, the mother has a right of self-defense in those rare cases where a child endangers her life.

Executive branch leaders in national health leadership positions have tyrannically controlled information, spent taxpayer funds, prioritized selfish gain, and controlled health care options to take healthcare decision-making freedom away from the people.

Executive branch leaders in the United States Department of Education have tyrannically and aggressively taken away parental and local government control over education.

Executive branch leaders have been given a continuously expanding budget that has immorally generated over 31 trillion dollars in national debt that rests on the backs of the American people. The tyrant demands more spending, but the moral response to debt is not higher debt ceilings and higher budgets, but the answer to this immoral and dangerous debt is to cut spending and actually pay off the debt itself.

We, therefore, appealing to the Supreme Judge of the World, resolve that the Congress of these United States should stand for a limited federal government, for a federal government primarily committed to protecting and defending the freedom of the people to have life, liberty, and the pursuit of happiness apart from tyranny, and we are committed to correcting tyranny in our federal executive branch and that we will use our Constitutional powers of oversight, budgeting, and impeachment to rid our federal government of foolish, deceitful, dangerous, criminal, and evil executive branch leaders who have proven by their conduct that their desire is for expansive federal government, not limited federal government. Our trust is in God, our commitment is to end tyranny in our United States Executive branch, and to these, we pledge our Service, our Influence, and our Sacred Honor.

About the Author

J. Stark Davis was raised in Morehead, Kentucky, where he attended K-12th grades at University Breckinridge School, graduating from high school in 1979. He then went to the United States Air Force Academy in Colorado Springs, Colorado, graduating in the Class of 1983 with a degree in International Affairs.

His active-duty time was spent as an Airborne Weapons Director onboard the E-3 aircraft, which included coastal defense work and deployments to Saudi Arabia, Iceland, and Okinawa; as an Instructor Weapons Director; and as a Wing Executive Officer for the Airborne Warning and Control System. His Air Force Reserve time began with work in a F-4 unit that was modernizing to F-16s, and ended with him serving as a USAF Academy Admissions Liaison Officer Director.

During his time in the Air Force Reserve, he also completed a law degree, built a successful private law practice, and served as a youth and family minister. After retiring from the Air Force as a Lieutenant Colonel he served as an AFJROTC Senior Aerospace Science Instructor in two public school systems and has taught criminal justice and law classes at two private Christian universities.

He has been married since 1988 to his wife Julie, they have 4 children.

Notes

Chapter 1

[1] Carl Sandburg, *Abraham Lincoln The War Years Volume One*, Harcourt, Brace, and Company, New York (1939), p. 584.

Chapter 2

[2] Ibid, p. 622.

Chapter 3

[3] Ibid, p. 620.

[4] Anna Giarittelli, "Suspected Terrorists Crossing Border 'At a Level We Have Never Seen Before,' Outgoing Border Patrol Chief Says," *Washington Examiner* (Aug. 16, 2021), https://www.washingtonexaminer.com/news/border-patrol-chief-suspected-terrorists-coming-across-southern-border (Sep. 1, 2023).

[5] U.S. Constitution, Article III, Section 3.

[6] Jessica M. Vaughan, "Biden's Border Policies Facilitate Shocking Modern Slavery," *New York Post* (Jan. 10, 2023), https://nypost.com/2023/01/10/bidens-border-policies-facilitate-shocking-modern-slavery/ (Sep. 1, 2023).

[7] Stephen Reinberg, "U.S. Deaths Due to Fentanyl Nearly Quadrupled in 5 Years," HealthDay, *US News* (May 3, 2023), https://www.usnews.com/news/health-news/articles/2023-05-03/u-s-deaths-due-to-fentanyl-nearly-quadrupled-in-5-years (Sep. 1, 2023).

[8] Virginia Allen, "New Data Reveals Number of Illegal Aliens Who Entered US Under Biden Exceeds Population of 22 States," *Microsoft Start* (Oct. 11, 2023), https://www.msn.com/en-us/news/us/new-data-reveals-number-of-illegal-aliens-who-entered-us-under-biden-exceeds-population-of-22-states/ar-AA1i3dBi (Sep. 2, 2023).

[9] Ryan Foley, "Border Patrol Reports Spike In Terror Watchlist suspects attempting to enter the US," *The Christian Post*, Thursday (Oct. 12, 2023), https://www.christianpost.com/news/border-patrol-reports-spike-in-terror-watchlist-suspects.html (Sep. 3).

[10] Mark Levin, "The Mark Levin Show" (Sep. 28, 2023), https://cumuluspodcastnetwork.com/pods/the-mark-levin-podcast/ (Sept. 29, 2023).

[11] Kendall v. United States ex Rel. Stokes, 37 U.S. 524 (1838).

[12] Kendall v. United States ex Rel. Stokes, 37 U.S. 524 (1838).

[13] Perry, O'Keefe and Montoya-Galvez, "Harris to Lead Administration's Efforts to Stem Migration at Border," *CBS News* (Mar. 24, 2021), https://www.cbsnews.com/news/kamala-harris-immigration-lead-mexico-border-biden-administration/ (Sept. 29, 2023)

Chapter 4

[14] Jason Fernando, "Gross National Product (GDP): Formula and How to Use It," *Investopedia* (Sept. 26, 2023), https://www.investopedia.com/terms/g/gdp.asp (Sept. 27, 2023).

[15] Kimberly Amadeo, "Who Owns the US National Debt?" *The Balance* (Jan. 19, 2023), https://www.thebalancemoney.com/who-owns-the-us-national-debt-3306124 (Sept. 27, 2023).

[16] "The Federal Budget in Fiscal Year 2022: An Infographic," Congressional Budget Office (Mar. 28, 2023), https://www.cbo.gov/publication/58888 (Sep. 27, 2023).

[17] Ibid.

[18] Kimberly Amadeo, "US National Debt by Year," *The Balance* (Jan. 18, 2023), https://www.thebalancemoney.com/national-debt-by-year-compared-to-gdp-and-major-events-3306287 (Sep. 27, 2023).

[19] Helen Dewar & Joan Biskupic, "Court Strikes Down Line-Item Veto," *Washington Post* (June 26, 1998), https://www.washingtonpost.com/wp-srv/national/longterm/supcourt/stories/wp062698.htm (Sep. 27. 2023).

[20] Tom Murse, "How Many Days a Year Congress Works," *ThoughtCo* (Feb. 3, 2020), https://www.thoughtco.com/average-number-of-legislative-days-3368250 (Sep. 27, 2023).

Chapter 5

[21] Vivek Saxena, "Kaleigh McEnany Faces Reality of Abortion Defeat, Suggests GOP Pass a Bunch of Dem-like Legislation," *American Wire*

(Nov. 8, 2023), https://americanwirenews.com/kayleigh-mcenany-faces-reality-of-abortion-defeat-suggest-gop-pass-a-bunch-of-dem-like-legislation/?utm_campaign=james&utm_content=11-8-23%20Daily%20AM&utm_medium=newsletter&utm_source=Get%20response&utm_term=email (Nov. 16, 2023).

[22] "Battle for Unborn Life Continues in Kentucky," *Liberty Counsel* (Nov. 21, 2022), https://lc.org/newsroom/details/112122-battle-for-unborn-life-continues-in-kentucky (Oct. 16, 2023).

[23] *Dobbs v. Jackson Women's Health Organization*, 142 S. Ct. 2228 (2022), 597 U.S. ___ (2022).

[24] "Women's Right to Know, Abortion & Pregnancy Risks," Louisiana Department of Health, https://ldh.la.gov/page/abortion-pregnancy-risks (Nov. 16, 2023).

[25] Katherine Kortsmit, Antoinette Tguyen, Michele Mandel, Elizabeth Clark, Lisa Hollier, Jessica Rodenhizer, and Maura Whiteman, "Abortion Surveillance—United States, 2020" CDC, Surveillance Summaries (Nov. 25, 2022), https://www.cdc.gov/mmwr/volumes/71/ss/ss7110a1.htm?s_cid=ss7110a1_w (Nov. 16, 2023).

[26] Christine Slomski, "Many Women Struggle Mentally After an Abortion. Few Counselors Know How to Help," Azcentral (Nov. 6, 2023), https://www.azcentral.com/story/opinion/op-ed/2023/11/06/abortion-impact-mental-health-counselors-training/71409485007/ (Nov. 16, 2023).

[27] Patty Knap, "Fathers of Aborted Children Feel Effects of the Crime," *National Catholic Register* (July 21, 2017), https://www.ncregister.com/blog/fathers-of-aborted-children-feel-effects-of-the-crime (Nov. 17, 2023).

Chapter 6

[28] Abraham Lincoln, *Lincoln on the Civil War: Selected Speeches*, Penguin Books (2011), p. 44.

[29] Eleanor Watson and David Martin, "Biden Announces U.S. Military Mission In Afghanistan Will End August 31," *CBS News* (July 9, 2021), https://www.cbsnews.com/news/biden-afghanistan-troop-withdrawal-2021-07-08/ (Oct. 5, 2023).

[30] W.J. Hennigan and Kimberly Dozier, "Joe Biden's Botched Withdrawal Plunges Afghanistan Into Chaos," *Time* (Aug. 15, 2021),

https://time.com/6090523/biden-afghanistan-withdrawal-taliban/ (Oct. 5, 2023).

[31] Steve Mollman, "Over 55 Nations Pitched in Against North Korea in the Korean War," *Quartz* (June 25, 2018), https://qz.com/1313317/over-55-nations-pitched-in-against-north-korea-in-the-korean-war (Oct. 17, 2023).

[32] "Biden: US Did Not Go to Afghanistan to 'Nation Build,' " *Deutche Well* (July 8, 2021), https://www.dw.com/en/biden-us-did-not-go-to-afghanistan-to-nation-build/a-58210503 (Oct. 17, 2023).

[33] W.J. Hennigan and Kimberly Dozier, "Joe Biden's Botched Withdrawal Plunges Afghanistan Into Chaos," *Time* (Aug. 15, 2021), https://time.com/6090523/biden-afghanistan-withdrawal-taliban/ (Oct. 5, 2023).

[34] C.V. Glines, "William 'Billy' Mitchell: Air Power Visionary," *HistoryNet* (June 12, 2006), https://www.historynet.com/william-billy-mitchell-an-air-power-visionary/ (Oct. 5, 2023).

[35] Scott Wong, "Veterans Deliver Emotional, Scathing Testimony About 'Disastrous' Afghanistan Withdrawal," *NBC News* (March 8, 2023), https://www.nbcnews.com/politics/congress/house-republicans-hearing-botched-afghanistan-withdrawal-biden-rcna73009 (Oct. 17, 2023).

Chapter 7

[36] "Code of Federal Regulations, Subchapter F, Part 101, Subpart D" CFR Title 14 (Oct. 19, 2023), https://www.ecfr.gov/current/title-14/chapter-I/subchapter-F/part-101/subpart-D (Oct. 23, 2023).

[37] Tom Vanden Brook, Josh Meyer, and Kevin Johnson, "Chinese Spy Balloon Sought Secret US Communications Signals, State Department Says," *USA Today* (Feb 9, 2023), https://www.usatoday.com/story/news/politics/2023/02/09/china-spy-balloon-sought-us-communications-state-department/11219163002/ (Oct. 19, 2023).

[38] John T. Correll, "Intercepting the Bear," *Air and Space Forces Magazine* (Feb. 26, 2018), https://www.airandspaceforces.com/article/intercepting-the-bear/ (Oct. 23, 2023).

[39] Ibid.

⁴⁰ Todd Vician, "How Does the U.S. Monitor Airspace Violations?" *World* (Feb. 25, 2023), https://wng.org/articles/how-does-the-u-s-monitor-airspace-violations-1675920830 (Oct. 23, 2023).

⁴¹ Rebecca Kheel, "DoD Struggles to Answer Questions on Chinese Balloon in Congressional Testimony," Military.com (Feb. 9, 2023), https://www.military.com/daily-news/2023/02/09/dod-struggles-answer-questions-chinese-balloon-congressional-testimony.html (Oct. 23, 2023).

⁴² Ibid.

⁴³ Tom Vanden Brook, Josh Meyer, and Kevin Johnson, "Chinese Spy Balloon Sought Secret US Communications Signals, State Department Says," *USA Today* (Feb 9, 2023), https://www.usatoday.com/story/news/politics/2023/02/09/china-spy-balloon-sought-us-communications-state-department/11219163002/ (Oct. 19, 2023).

Chapter 8

⁴⁴ Olivia Land, "Hamas Kills 40 Babies and Children—Beheading Some of Them—At Israeli Kibbutz: Report," *New York Post* (Oct. 10, 2023), https://nypost.com/2023/10/10/hamas-kills-40-babies-and-children-beheading-some-of-them-at-israeli-kibbutz-report/ (Oct. 20, 2023).

⁴⁵ Chris Pandolfo, Elisabeth Pritchett, Gabriele Regalbuto, Louis Casiano, Kassy Dillon, Adam Sabes and Brandon Gillespie, "HAMAS Releases Two American Hostages, a Mother and Daughter, As Israel Continues Gaza Bombardment," *Fox News* (Oct. 20, 2023), https://www.foxnews.com/live-news/october-20-israel-hamas-war (Oct. 20, 2023).

⁴⁶ Richard Overy, "Goodbye to the 'Nazi's'," *History Today* (May 5, 2013), https://www.historytoday.com/goodbye-nazis (Oct. 22, 2023).

⁴⁷ Kim Ghattas, "A Message From Iran," *The Atlantic* (Oct. 8, 2023), https://www.theatlantic.com/international/archive/2023/10/iran-hamas-israel-gaza-attack/675582/ (Oct. 21, 2023).

⁴⁸ "Obama Administration Acknowledges $1.7B Transfer to Iran Was All Cash," *CBS News* (Sep. 6, 2016), https://www.cbsnews.com/news/obama-administration-acknowledges-1-7-billion-transfer-to-iran-was-all-cash/ (Oct. 21, 2023).

⁴⁹ Adam Kredo, "Iran Has Made $80 Billion in Illicit Oil Sales Since Biden Took Office," *The Washington Free Beacon* (Oct. 10, 2023),

https://freebeacon.com/national-security/iran-has-made-80-billion-in-illicit-oil-sales-since-biden-took-office/ (Oct. 22, 2023).
[50] Ibid.

Chapter 9

[51] Reena Flores, "FBI Releases Documents from Hillary Clinton Email Investigation," *CBS News* (Sept. 2, 2023), https://www.cbsnews.com/news/fbi-releases-documents-from-hillary-clinton-email-investigation/
[52] Reena Flores, "FBI Releases Documents from Hillary Clinton Email Investigation," CBS News, Politics, https://www.cbsnews.com/news/fbi-releases-documents-from-hillary-clinton-email-investigation/ (Oct. 16, 2023).
[53] Samuel Chamberlain and Steven Nelson, "FBI, DOJ's Trump-Russia 'Collusion' Probe was 'Seriously Flawed,' No Basis in Evidence When Opened:," *New York Post* (May 15, 2023), https://nypost.com/2023/05/15/fbi-doj-failed-to-observe-fidelity-to-the-law-in-trump-russia-investigation-durham/ (Oct. 16, 2023).
[54] Matt Vespa, "Flynn Exonerated: DOJ Drops Charges After FBI Entrapment Plot Exposed," *Townhall* (May 7, 2020. https://townhall.com/tipsheet/mattvespa/2020/05/07/doj-dropping-case-against-michael-flynn-n2568403 (Oct. 16, 2023).
[55] Federal Prosecution of Election Offenses, Election Crimes Branch, DOJ, 2017. https://www.justice.gov/criminal-pin/election-crimes-branch (Oct. 16, 2023).
[56] Ibid.
[57] Ibid.
[58] "Voter Fraud Convictions in the 2016-2020 Elections," The A-Mark Foundation, (Sept. 11, 2023), https://the2020election.org/voter-fraud-convictions-since-2016/pennsylvania/ (Oct. 16, 2023).
[59] Press Releases, FBI, https://www.fbi.gov/news/press-releases (Aug. 1, 2021).
[60] Aleks Phillips, "Full List of Capital Rioters Jailed So Far and the Sentences They are Serving," *Newsweek* (Sept. 12, 2023), https://www.newsweek.com/full-list-capitol-rioters-jailed-sentences-january-6-1826075 (Oct. 24, 2023).

61 Hans A. von Spakovsky and Katie Samalis-Adrich, "Election Fraud Database Tops 1,400 Cases," *The Heritage Foundation* (Jan 18, 2023), https://www.heritage.org/election-integrity/commentary/election-fraud-database-tops-1400-cases (Oct. 24, 2023).

62 Robert Epstein, "Epstein: Google is Shifting Votes on a Massive Scale, But a Solution Is At Hand," *Daily Caller* (Nov. 6, 2022), https://dailycaller.com/2022/11/06/robert-epstein-2022-midterm-elections-google-bing/ (Oct. 24, 2023).

63 Joe Bukuras, "Acquitted Pro-Life Activist Mark Houck Reveals Details of 'Reckless' FBI Raid; Will Press Charges," *Catholic News Agency* (Feb.1, 2023), https://www.catholicnewsagency.com/news/253523/acquitted-pro-life-activist-mark-houck-reveals-details-of-fbi-raid-will-press-charges (Oct. 26, 2023).

64 Jesse O'Neill, "Virginia Woman Says FBI Staked Out School Board Meeting," *New York Post* (Oct. 27, 2021), https://nypost.com/2021/10/27/virginia-woman-says-fbi-staked-out-school-board-meeting/ (Oct. 26, 2023).

65 Victor Nava, "Dozens of FBI Sources Gave 'Criminal information' on Bidens that DOJ Tried to Discredit as 'Foreign Disinformation': Grassley," *New York Post* (Oct. 25, 2023), https://nypost.com/2023/10/25/news/fbi-had-over-40-confidential-sources-providing-criminal-information-on-biden-family-sen-chuck-grassley-says/ (Oct. 26, 2023).

66 Ibid.

67 Rachel Treisman, "These Are the Charges Trump Was Indicted On and What They Mean," *NPR* (June 9, 2023), https://www.npr.org/2023/06/09/1181340894/trump-indictment-classified-documents-charges (Oct. 26, 2023).

Chapter 10

68 Eric Scheiner, "Unhappy Anniversary: Biden Killed Keystone Pipeline 3 Years Ago," *MRC TV* (Jan. 20, 2024), https://www.mrctv.org/blog/eric-scheiner/unhappy-anniversary-biden-killed-keystone-pipeline-3-years-ago (Jan. 22, 2024).

69 Executive Order 13990, "Protecting Public Health and the Environment and Restoring Science To Tackle the Climate Crisis," *Federal Register* (Jan. 25, 2021),

https://www.federalregister.gov/documents/2021/01/25/2021-01765/protecting-public-health-and-the-environment-and-restoring-science-to-tackle-the-climate-crisis (Feb. 7, 2024).

[70] Ibid.

[71] Ibid

[72] Andrew Chatzky, Anshu Siripurapu, "Envisioning a Green New Deal: A Global Comparison," Council of Foreign Relations (Feb1, 2021), https://www.cfr.org/backgrounder/envisioning-green-new-deal-global-comparison (Feb. 25, 2024).

[73] Ibid.

[74] Ibid.

[75] Nathan Rott, "Biden Moves To Have U.S. Rejoin Climate Accord," NPR (Jan. 20, 2021), https://www.npr.org/sections/inauguration-day-live-updates/2021/01/20/958923821/biden-moves-to-have-u-s-rejoin-climate-accord (Feb. 25, 2024).

Chapter 11

[76] Madison Czopek, "House Republicans' Findings About the Biden Family's Foreign Business Practices, Explained," *PolitiFact* (May 16, 2023), https://www.politifact.com/article/2023/may/16/house-republicans-findings-about-the-biden-familys/ (Oct. 27, 2023).

[77] Annie Grayer, "House Oversight GOP Claims They Don't Need to Find Direct Payments to Joe Biden to Prove Corruption in Hunter Biden Business Dealings Memo," *CNN* (Aug. 9, 2023), https://www.cnn.com/2023/08/09/politics/house-oversight-republicans-hunter-biden/index.html (Oct. 27, 2023).

[78] Steven Nelson, "Biden $10M Bribe File Released: Burisma Chief Said He Was 'Coerced' to pay Joe, 'Stupid' Hunter In Bombshell Allegations," *New York Post* (July 20, 2023), https://nypost.com/2023/07/20/biden-bribe-file-released-burisma-chief-said-both-joe-and-hunter-involved/ (Oct. 27, 2023).

[79] Lauren Camera, "Biden's $6 Billion Burden," US News (Oct. 13, 2023), https://www.usnews.com/news/politics/articles/2023-10-13/despite-state-department-assurances-6b-in-iran-funds-leaves-white-house-vulnerable (Oct. 14, 2023).

Chapter 12

[80] "Is a Transgender Woman Still Genetically Male After Surgery?" *The Tech Interactive* (Mar. 18, 2020), https://www.thetech.org/ask-a-geneticist/articles/2020/transgender-genetics/ (Oct. 30, 2023).

[81] Mark Moore and Samuel Chamberlain, "Judge Jackson Defines to Define 'Woman,' Says She's 'Not a Biologist'," *New York Post* (Mar. 23, 20220, https://nypost.com/2022/03/23/sen-blackburn-slams-judge-jackson-on-definition-of-woman/ (Oct. 29, 2023).

[82] Ryan T. Anderson, "Sex Reassignment Doesn't Work. Here is the Evidence," *The Heritage Foundation* (Mar 9, 2018), https://www.heritage.org/gender/commentary/sex-reassignment-doesnt-work-here-the-evidence (Oct. 30, 2023).

[83] Ed Komenda, "Trans Minors Protected From Parents Under Washington Law," AP (May 9, 2023), https://apnews.com/article/washington-transgender-health-care-minors-parents-296005ba7c084db94e241283067d2dff (Nov. 17, 2023).

[84] Kimberly Fletcher, "Parents Must Stand Up Against Gender Surgeries Performed on Minors," Newsweek (Oct. 17, 2023), https://www.msn.com/en-us/health/medical/parents-must-stand-up-against-gender-surgeries-performed-on-minors-opinion/ar-AA1gWvUW (Nov. 17, 2023).

Chapter 13

[85] Debate at Alton, Illinois, Oct. 15, 1858 (CWAL III:310)

[86] Kimberly Amadeo, "How Outsourcing Jobs Affects the U.S. Economy," *The Balance* (June 16, 2022), https://www.thebalancemoney.com/how-outsourcing-jobs-affects-the-u-s-economy-3306279 (Oct. 31, 2023).

[87] Jason Lemon, "China Increasing Military Capability at 'Serious and Sustained Rate,' Top U.S. General Says," (June 10, 2021), https://www.newsweek.com/china-increasing-military-capability-serious-sustained-rate-top-us-general-says-1599478 (Nov. 2, 2023).

[88] Dan Price, "7 Reasons TikTok is Bad for Everyone," Make Use Of (Sept. !6, 2023), https://www.makeuseof.com/is-tiktok-bad/ (Nov. 2, 2023).

[89] Philip Lenczycki, "Exclusive: Chinese Parent of US Battery Maker Has Business Ties with Blacklisted CCP Paramilitary Group," *Daily Caller* (Oct. 30, 2023), https://dailycaller.com/2023/10/30/gotion-china-blacklisted-ccp-group/ (Nov. 1, 2023).

90 Ibid.

91 Ibid.

92 Ibid.

93 Ibid.

94 Ibid.

95 Charlie McCarthy, "Disney Stock at 9-Year Low, Anti-woke Boycott Continues," *Newsmax* (Aug. 28, 2023), https://www.newsmax.com/newsfront/walt-disney-company-woke-stock-price/2023/08/28/id/1132366/ (Nov. 3, 2023).

96 The Associated Press, "Bud Light Sales Plunged After Boycott Over Campaign With Transgender Influencer, Company Reveals," *The Associated Press* (Aug. 3, 2023), https://www.nbcnews.com/business/business-news/bud-light-sales-plunged-boycott-campaign-transgender-influencer-compan-rcna97944 (Nov. 3, 2023).

97 F. John Reh, "Pros and Cons of Offshoring," *The Balance* (Sept. 13, 2022), https://www.thebalancemoney.com/offshoring-smart-business-or-shortsightedness-2275188 (Oct. 31, 2023).

98 Robert Epstein, "Epstein: Google is Shifting Votes on a Massive Scale, But a Solution Is At Hand," *Daily Caller* (Nov. 6, 2022), https://dailycaller.com/2022/11/06/robert-epstein-2022-midterm-elections-google-bing/ (Oct. 24, 2023).

99 Hayden Ludwig, "CTCL's 'Zuck Bucks' Invade Michigan and Wisconsin," Capital Research Center (Feb. 3, 2021), https://capitalresearch.org/article/ctcls-zuck-bucks-invade-michigan-and-wisconsin/ (Nov. 3, 2021).

Chapter 14

100 Danielle DeSimone, "Over 200 Years of Service: The History of Women in the U.S. Military," USO (Feb. 28, 2023), https://www.uso.org/stories/3005-over-200-years-of-service-the-history-of-women-in-the-us-military (Nov. 5, 2023).

101 R.J. Tobia, "Defense Secretary Carter Opens All Combat Jobs to Women," *PBS News Hour* (Dec. 3, 2015), https://www.pbs.org/newshour/nation/watch-live-defense-secretary-carter-to-lift-ban-on-women-in-combat-jobs (Nov. 3, 2023).

[102] Rostker v. Goldberg, 453 U.S. 57 (1981), *Justia*, https://supreme.justia.com/cases/federal/us/453/57/ (Nov. 3, 2023).

[103] Christian Shields, "Former NCAA Swimmer Speaks on Defending Women's Sports Amidst Cultural Confusion," Liberty University (April 14, 2023), https://www.liberty.edu/news/2023/04/14/former-ncaa-swimmer-speaks-on-defending-womens-sports-amidst-cultural-confusion/ (Nov. 5, 2023).

www.ingramcontent.com/pod-product-compliance
Lightning Source LLC
LaVergne TN
LVHW061549070526
838199LV00077B/6961